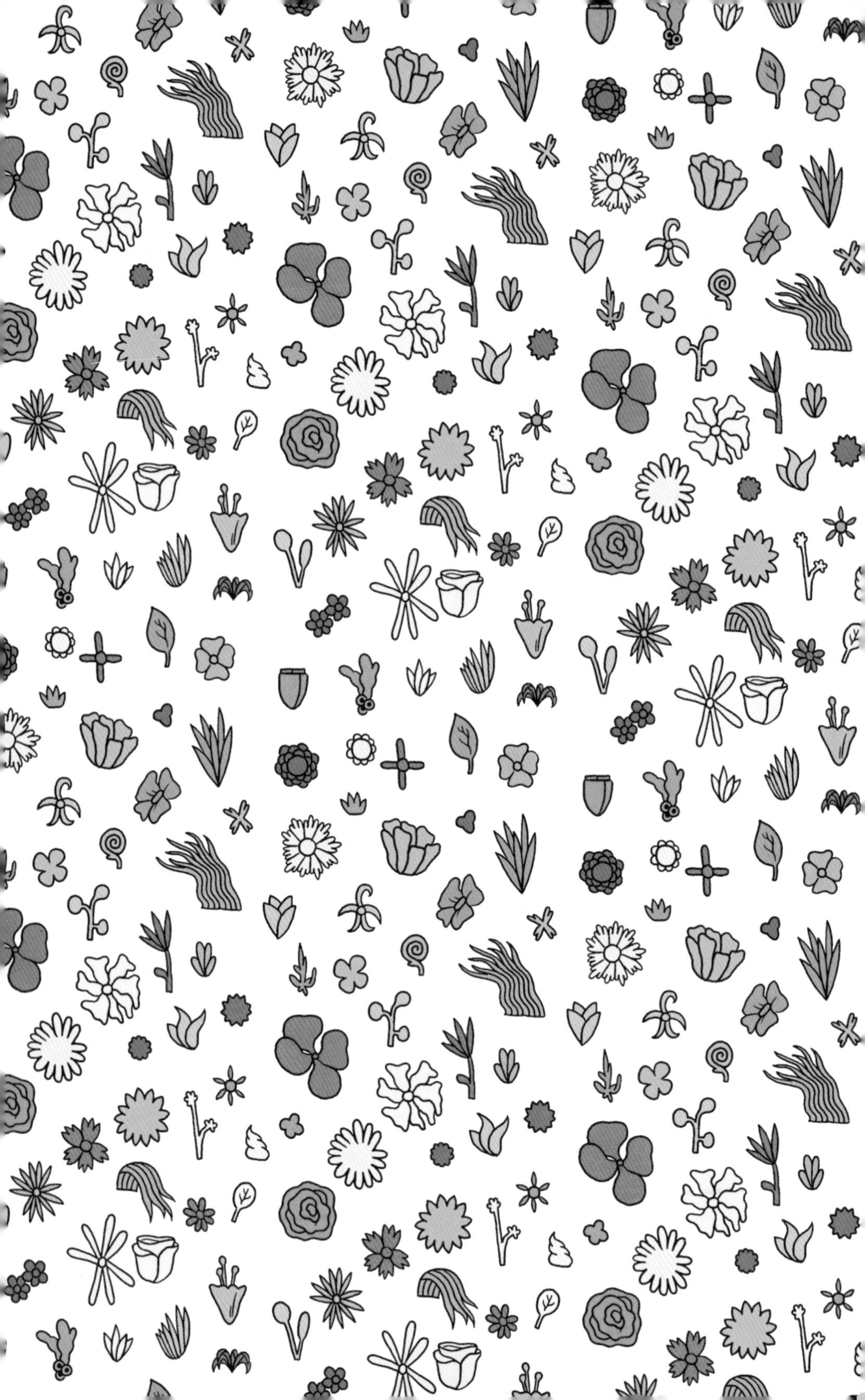

First year healthy

Drawn & Quarterly

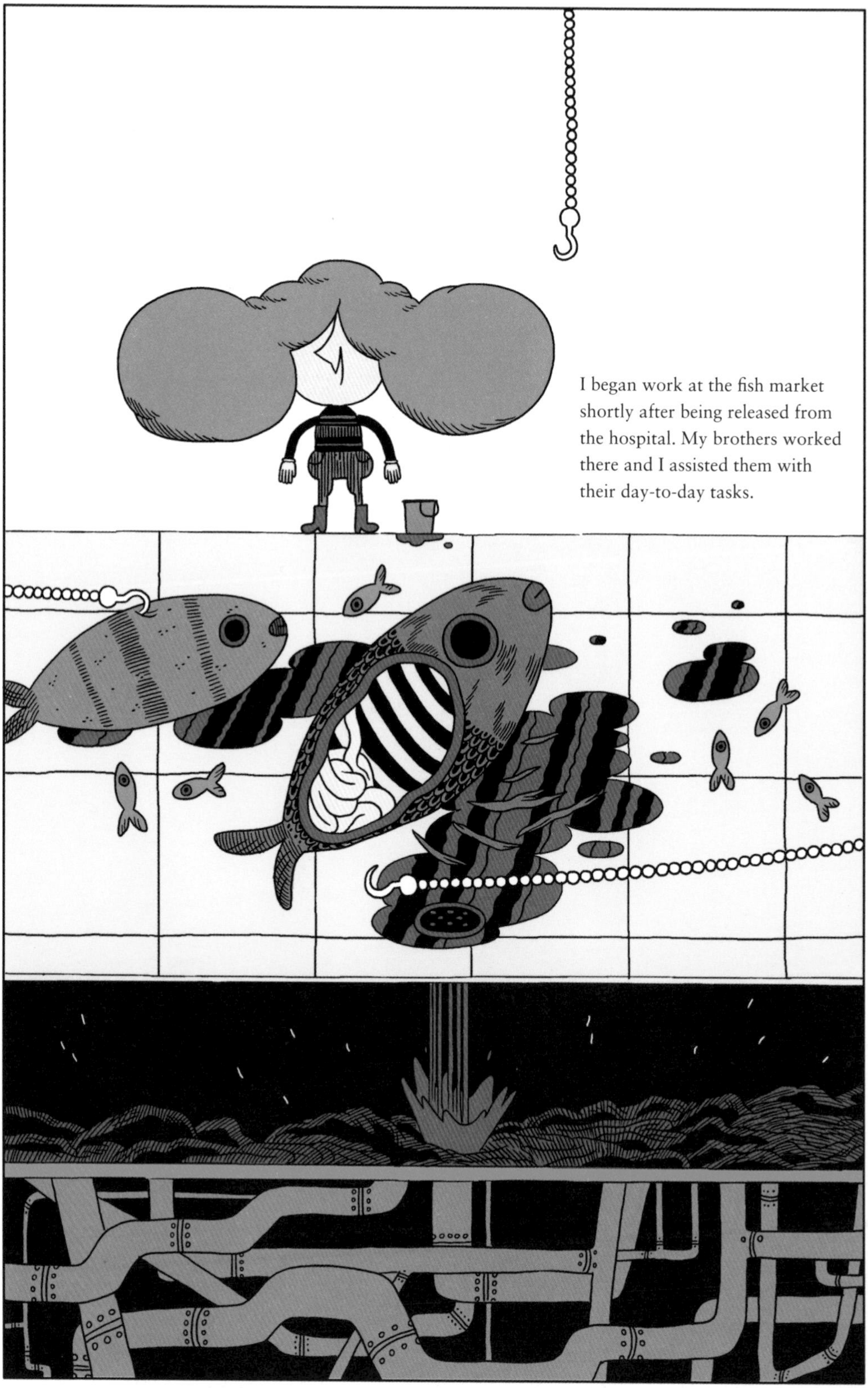
I began work at the fish market shortly after being released from the hospital. My brothers worked there and I assisted them with their day-to-day tasks.

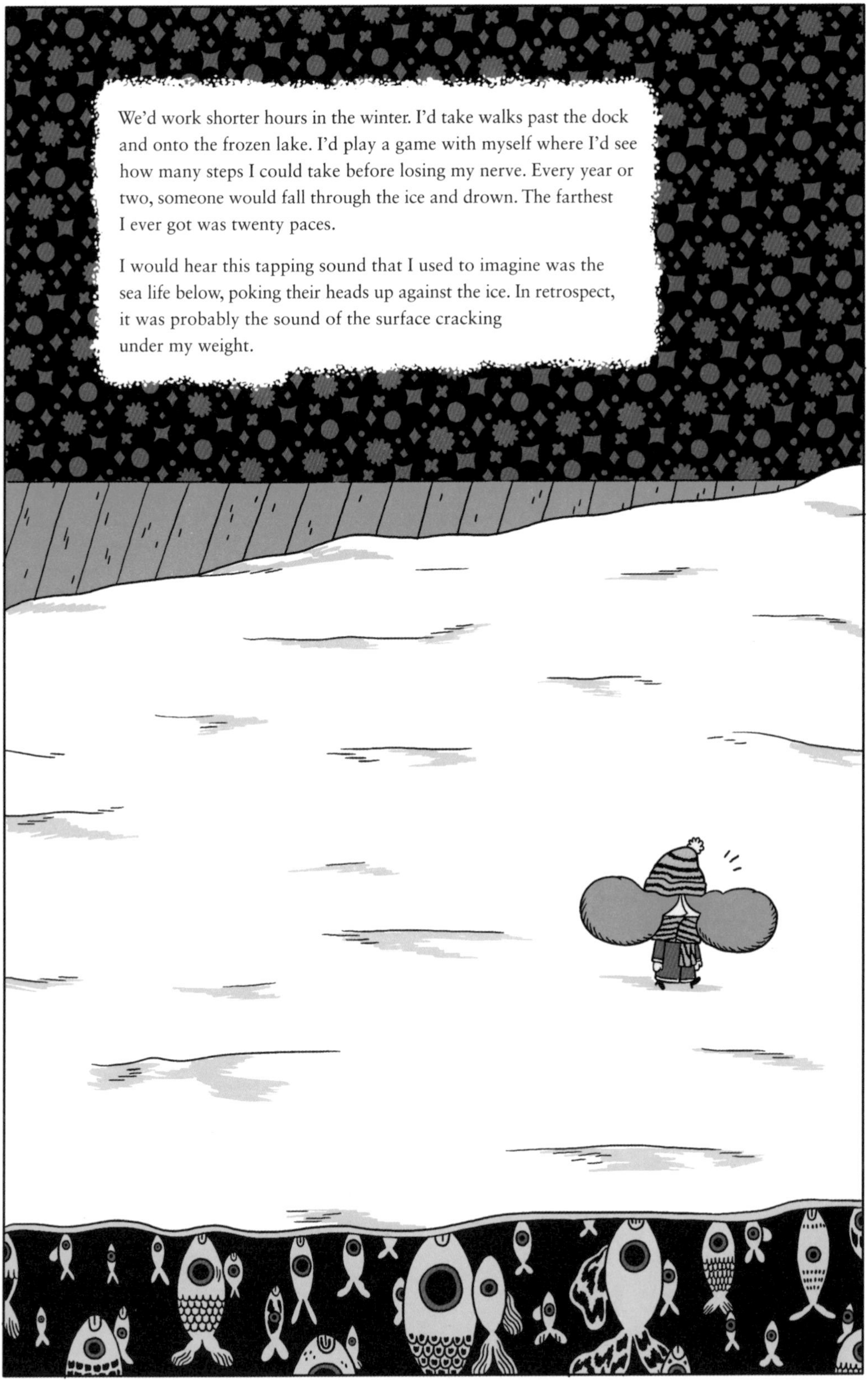
We'd work shorter hours in the winter. I'd take walks past the dock and onto the frozen lake. I'd play a game with myself where I'd see how many steps I could take before losing my nerve. Every year or two, someone would fall through the ice and drown. The farthest I ever got was twenty paces.
I would hear this tapping sound that I used to imagine was the sea life below, poking their heads up against the ice. In retrospect, it was probably the sound of the surface cracking under my weight.

The shorter shifts meant that I could spend time with another market employee—a Turk, two years my senior. We would take long lunches outside. We started playing this game where we would bet on whether or not it was too cold for him to get hard and jack off outside. He'd have to do it fast or he'd get frostbite on his thighs. Then we'd bet on how many seconds it would take for his mess to freeze on the snow.

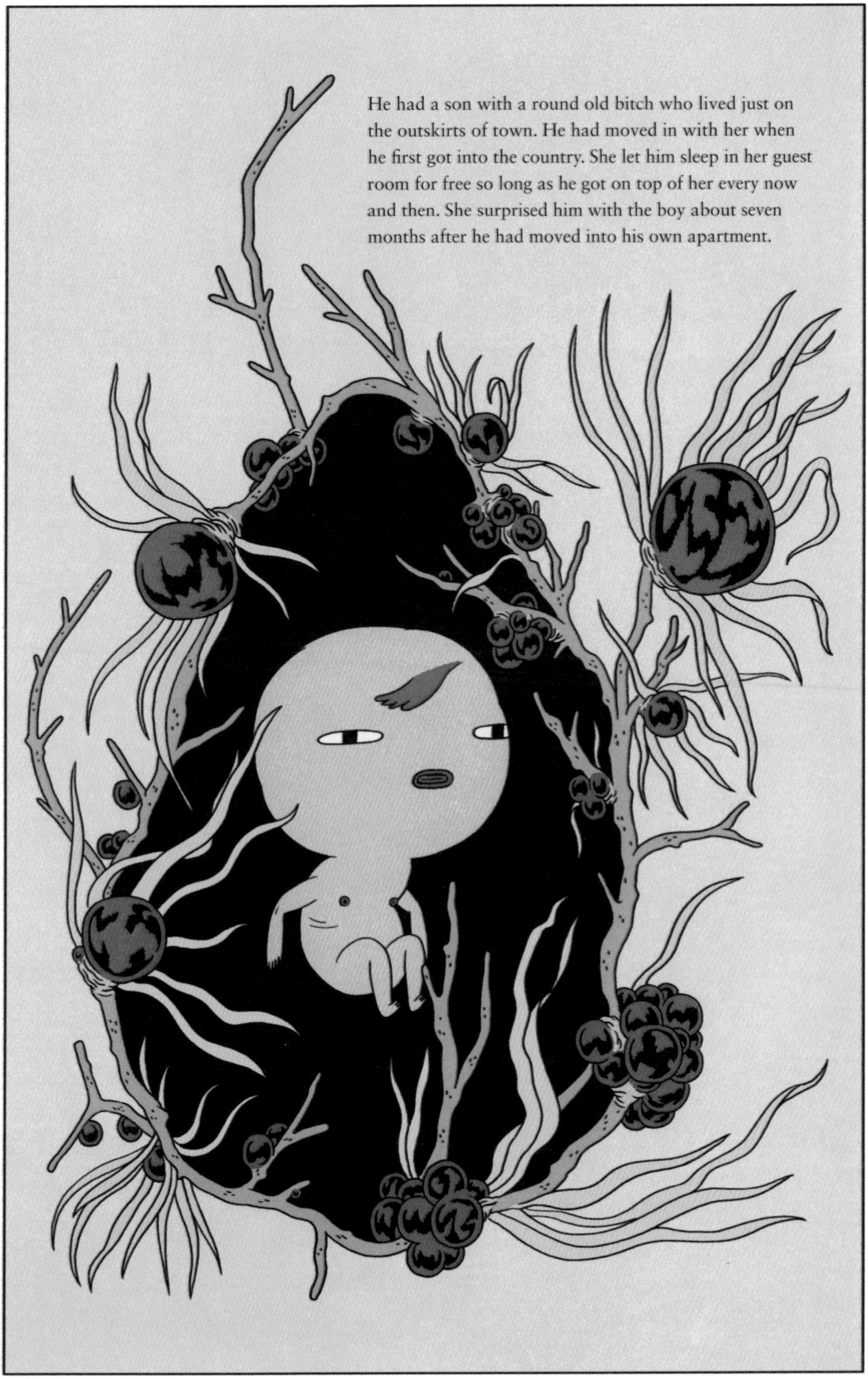
He had a son with a round old bitch who lived just on the outskirts of town. He had moved in with her when he first got into the country. She let him sleep in her guest room for free so long as he got on top of her every now and then. She surprised him with the boy about seven months after he had moved into his own apartment.

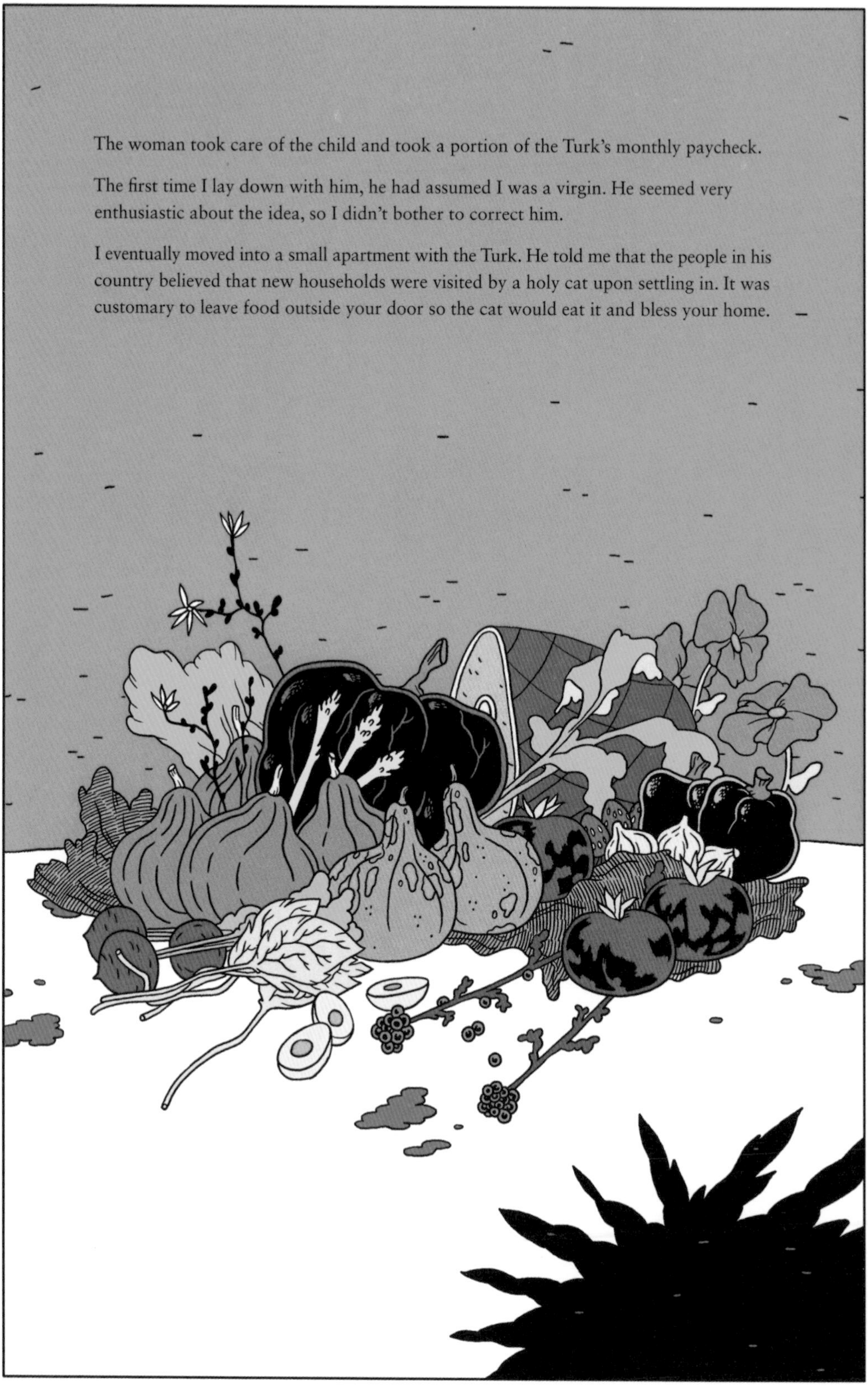
The woman took care of the child and took a portion of the Turk's monthly paycheck.
The first time I lay down with him, he had assumed I was a virgin. He seemed very enthusiastic about the idea, so I didn't bother to correct him.
I eventually moved into a small apartment with the Turk. He told me that the people in his country believed that new households were visited by a holy cat upon settling in. It was customary to leave food outside your door so the cat would eat it and bless your home.

I dreamt about the cat later that night. It wasn't moving or doing anything much at all.

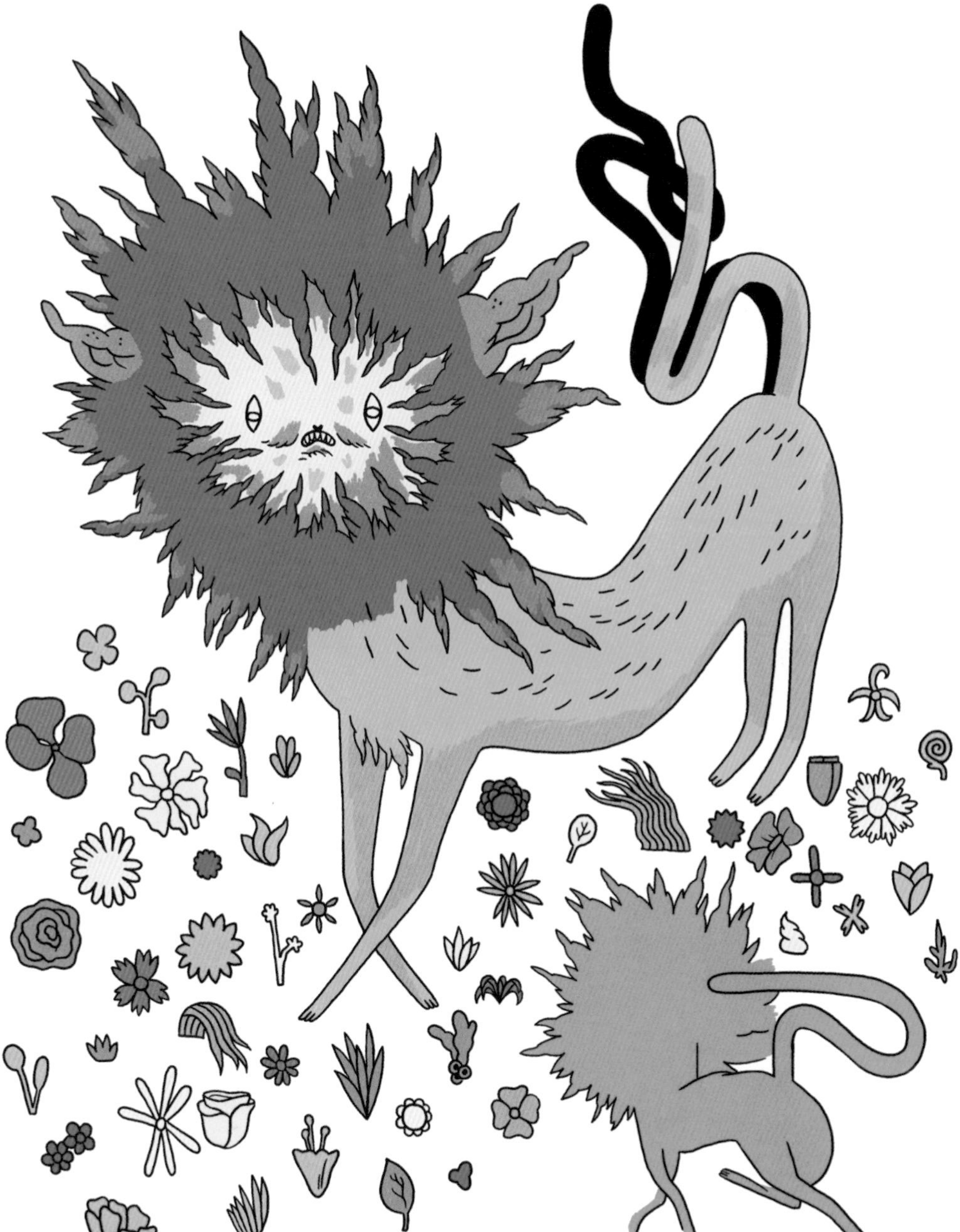

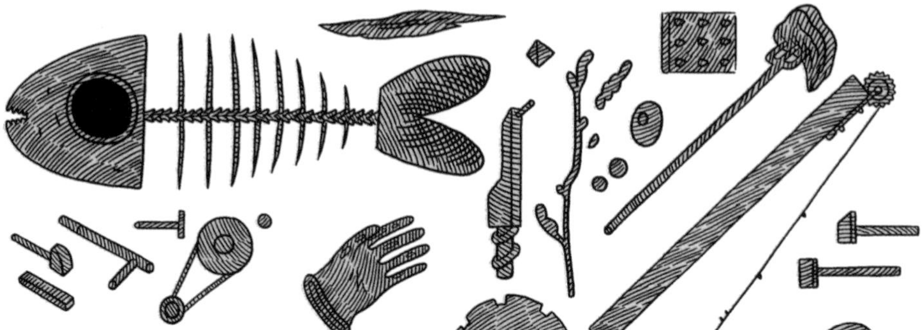

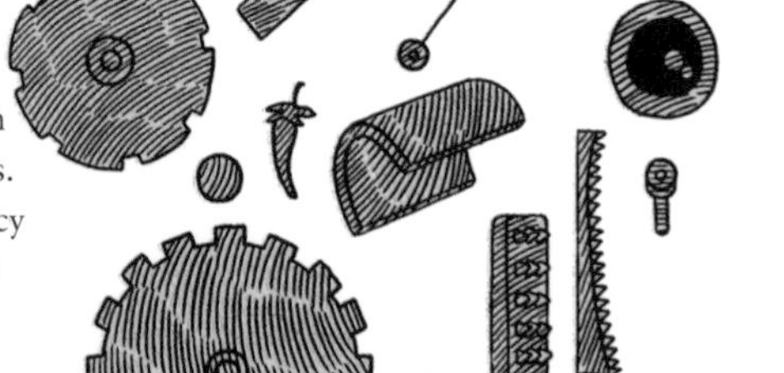

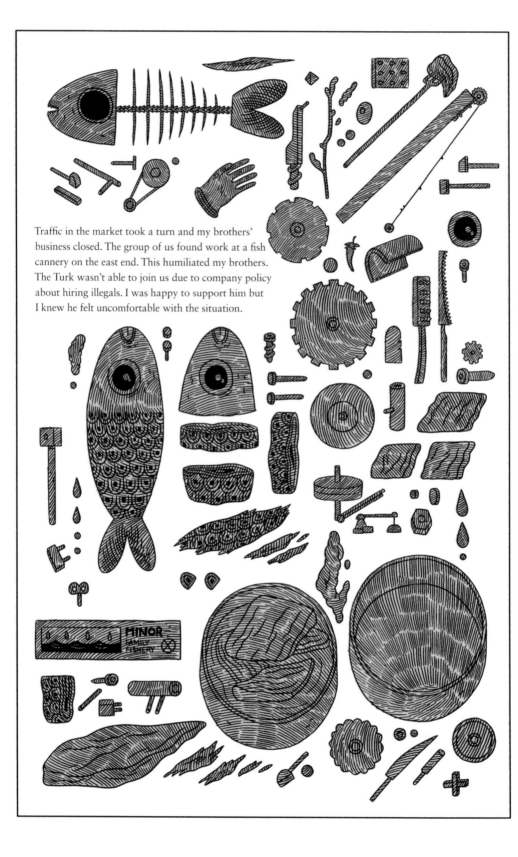

Traffic in the market took a turn and my brothers' business closed. The group of us found work at a fish cannery on the east end. This humiliated my brothers. The Turk wasn't able to join us due to company policy about hiring illegals. I was happy to support him but I knew he felt uncomfortable with the situation.

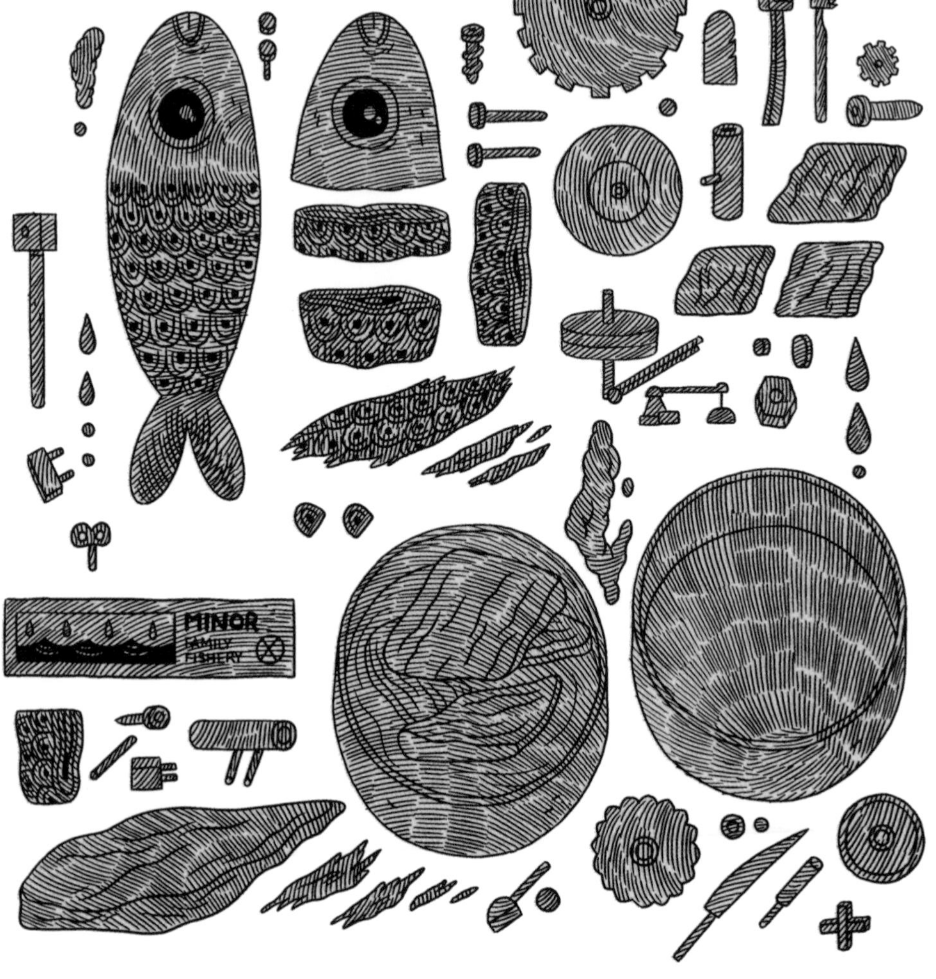
MINOR
FAMILY
FISHERY

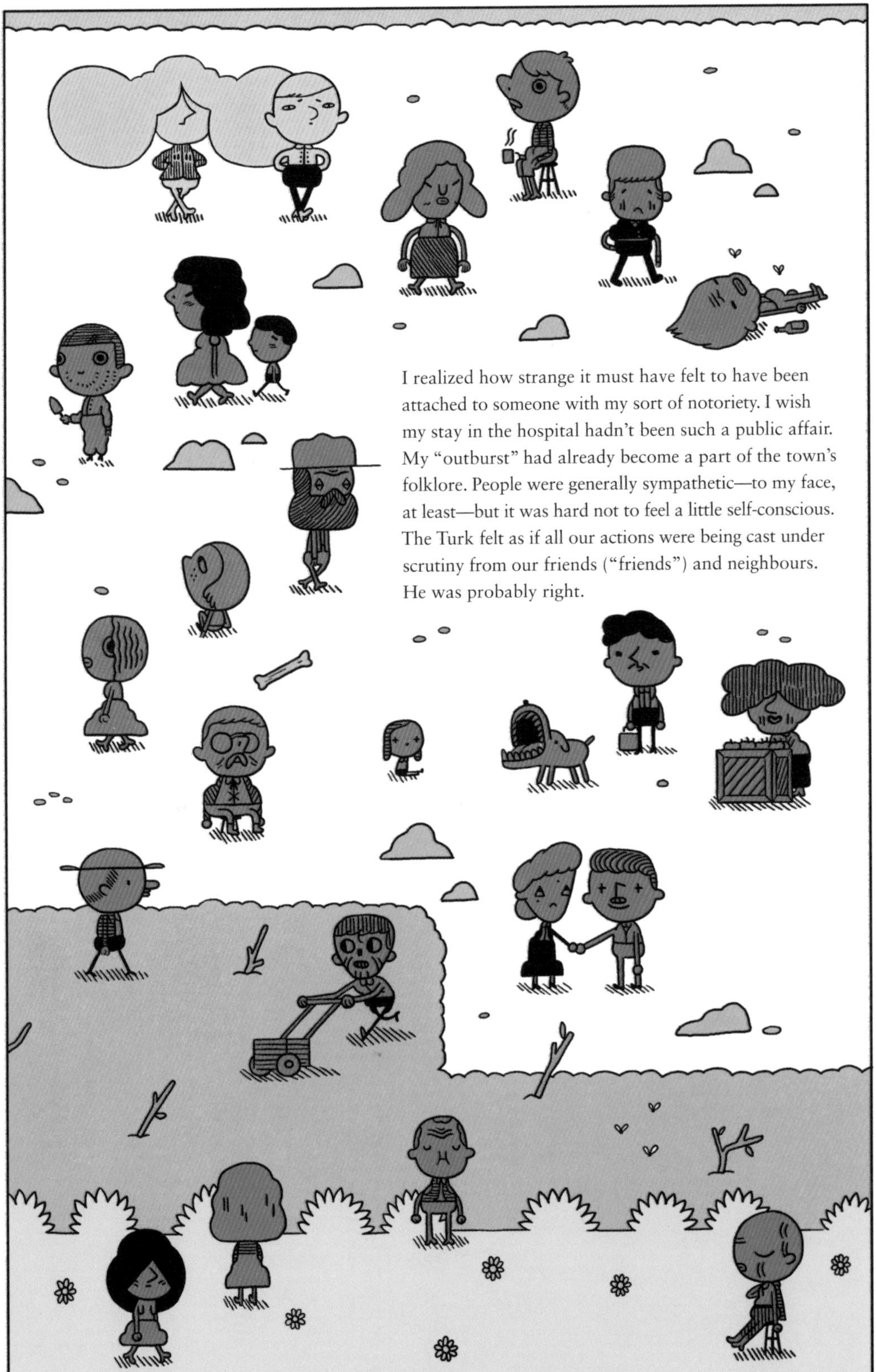
I realized how strange it must have felt to have been attached to someone with my sort of notoriety. I wish my stay in the hospital hadn't been such a public affair. My "outburst" had already become a part of the town's folklore. People were generally sympathetic—to my face, at least—but it was hard not to feel a little self-conscious. The Turk felt as if all our actions were being cast under scrutiny from our friends ("friends") and neighbours. He was probably right.

The Turk had a friend in Sudbury who he knew from the old country. He was involved in various low-level criminal enterprises: gambling rings, smuggling—that sort of thing. The Turk began to work alongside him. It was a long commute to the city. He would leave our apartment very early in the morning and come home very late at night.

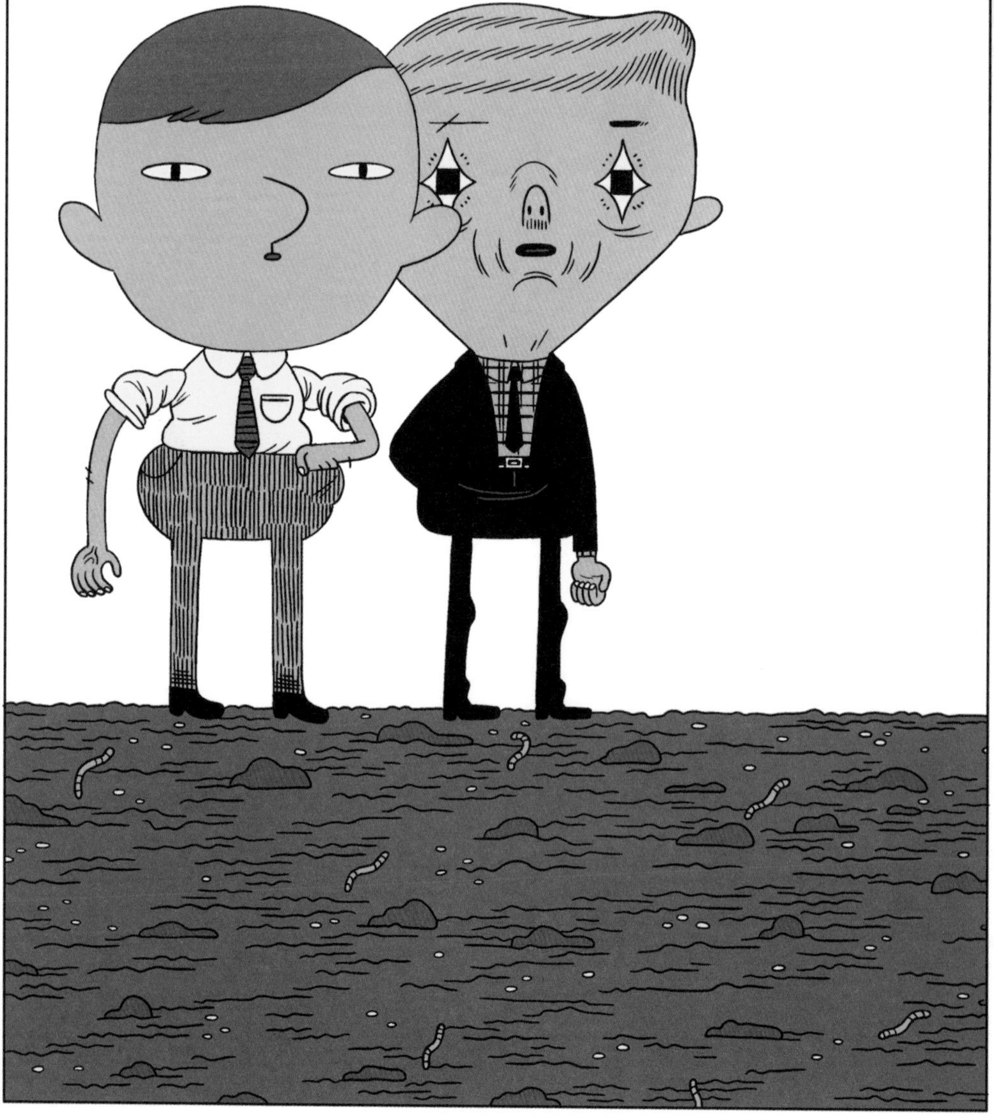

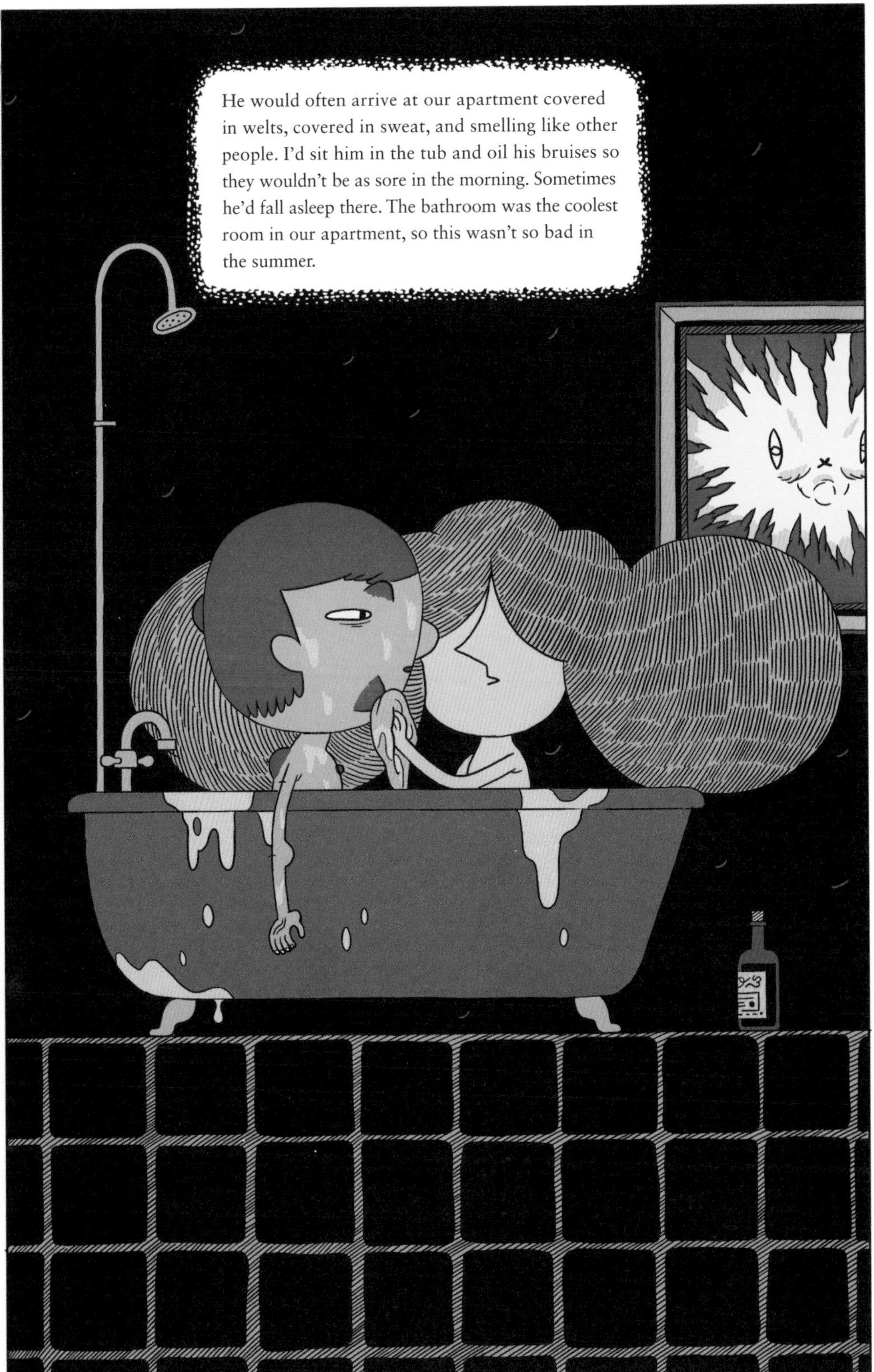
He would often arrive at our apartment covered in welts, covered in sweat, and smelling like other people. I'd sit him in the tub and oil his bruises so they wouldn't be as sore in the morning. Sometimes he'd fall asleep there. The bathroom was the coolest room in our apartment, so this wasn't so bad in the summer.

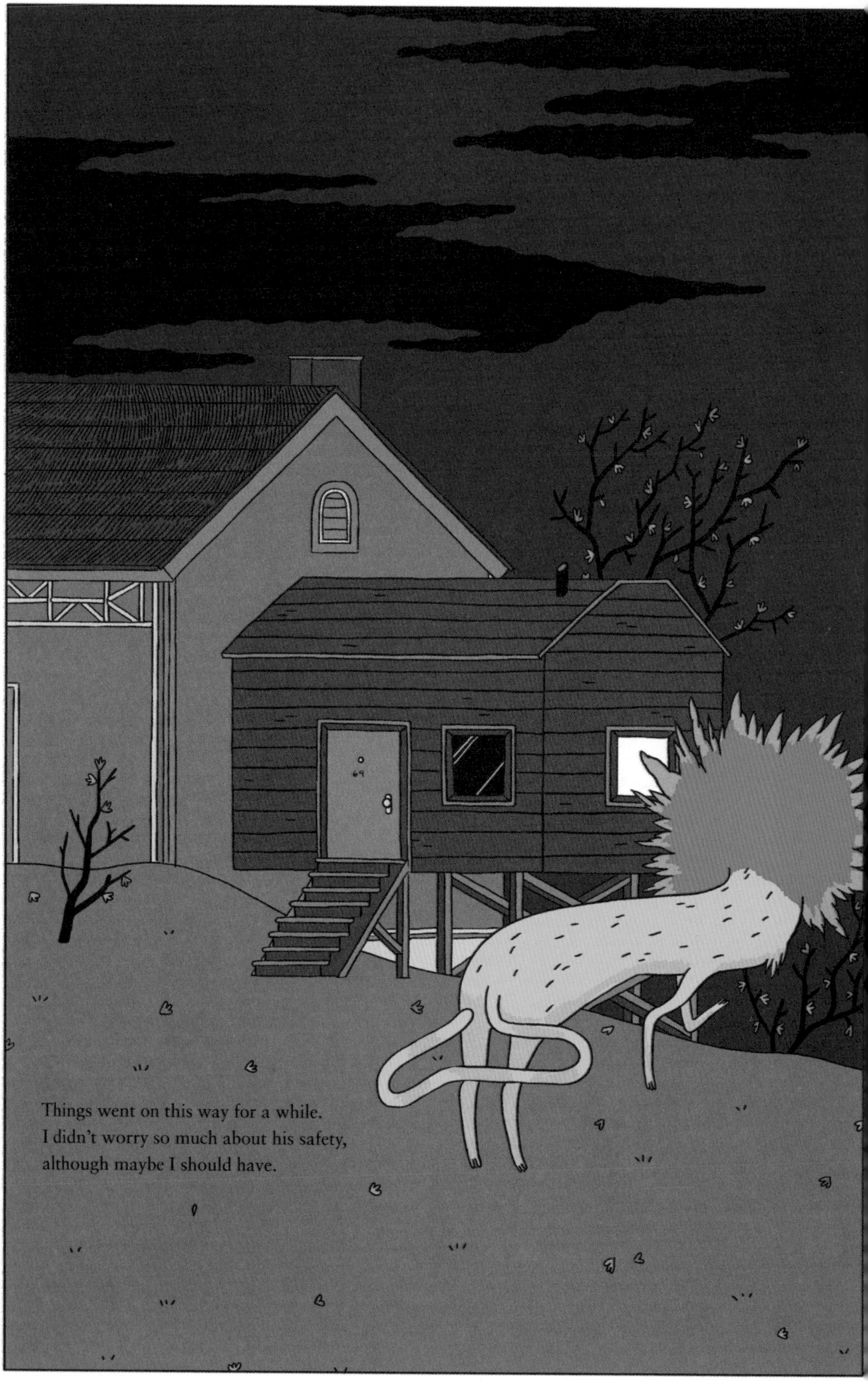
Things went on this way for a while.
I didn't worry so much about his safety,
although maybe I should have.

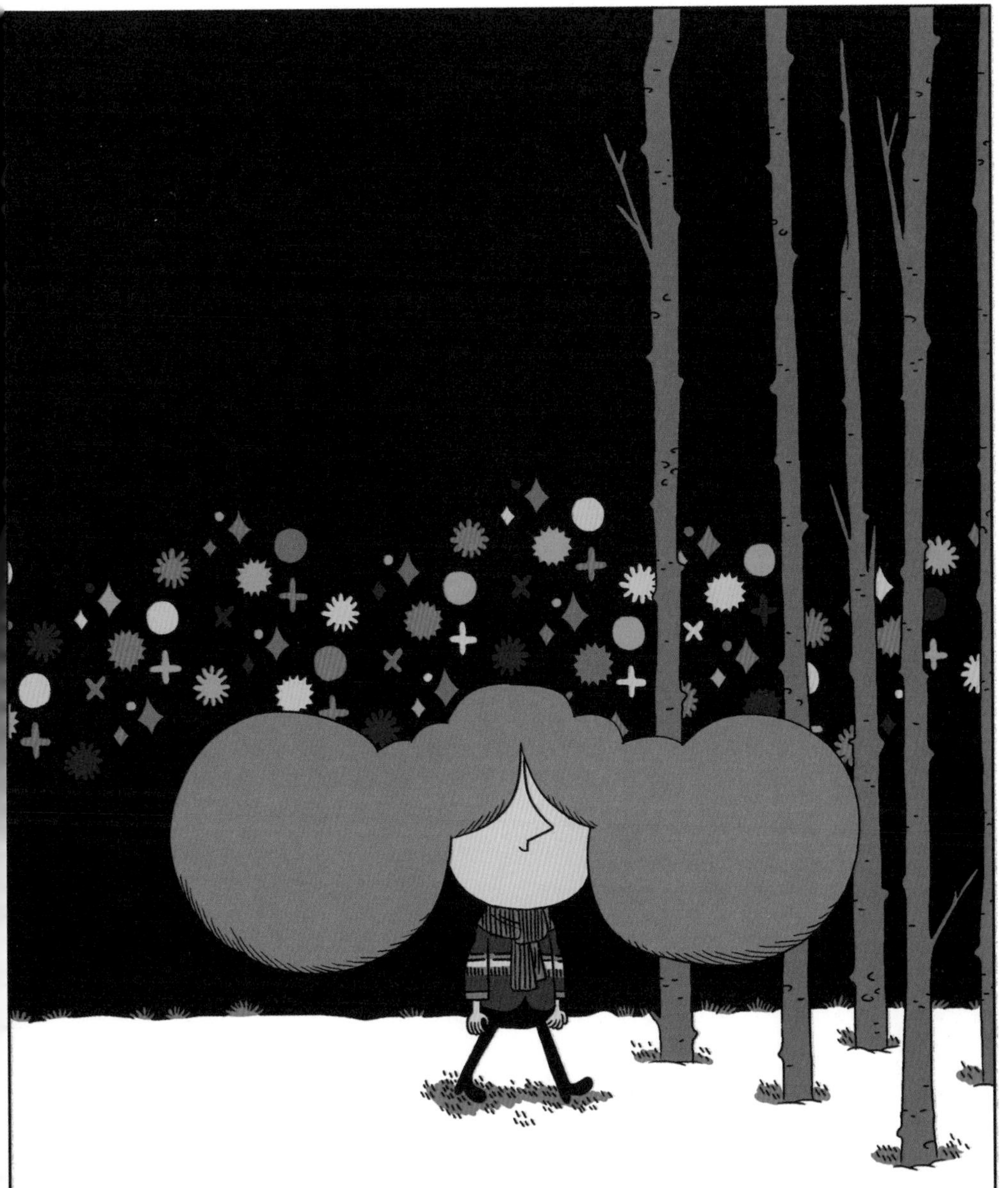

He was making enough money to support the two of us on his own, but I wanted to keep working. One of the nuns who had taken care of me at the hospital had recommended that keeping my days full and busy would help fend off future episodes.

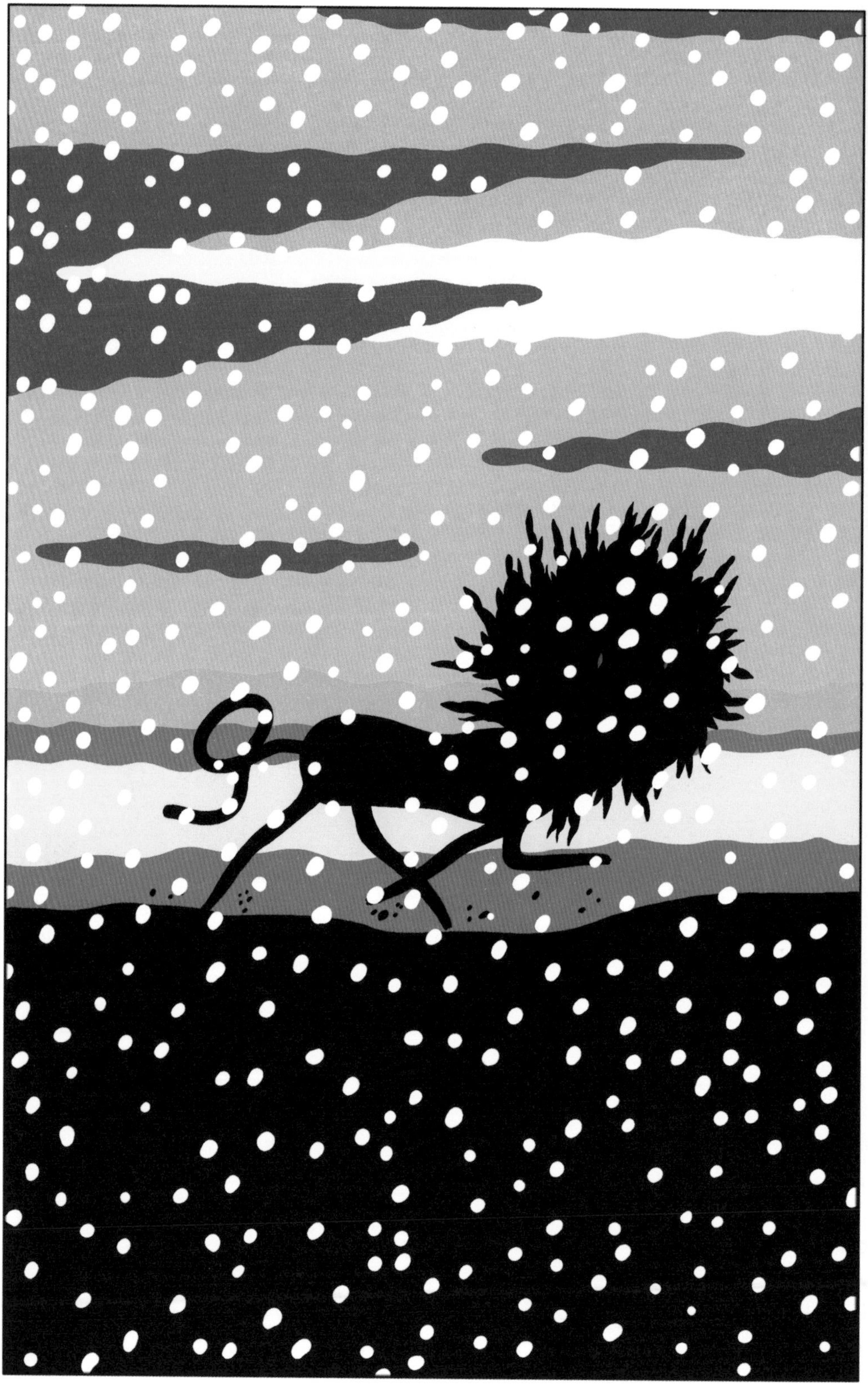

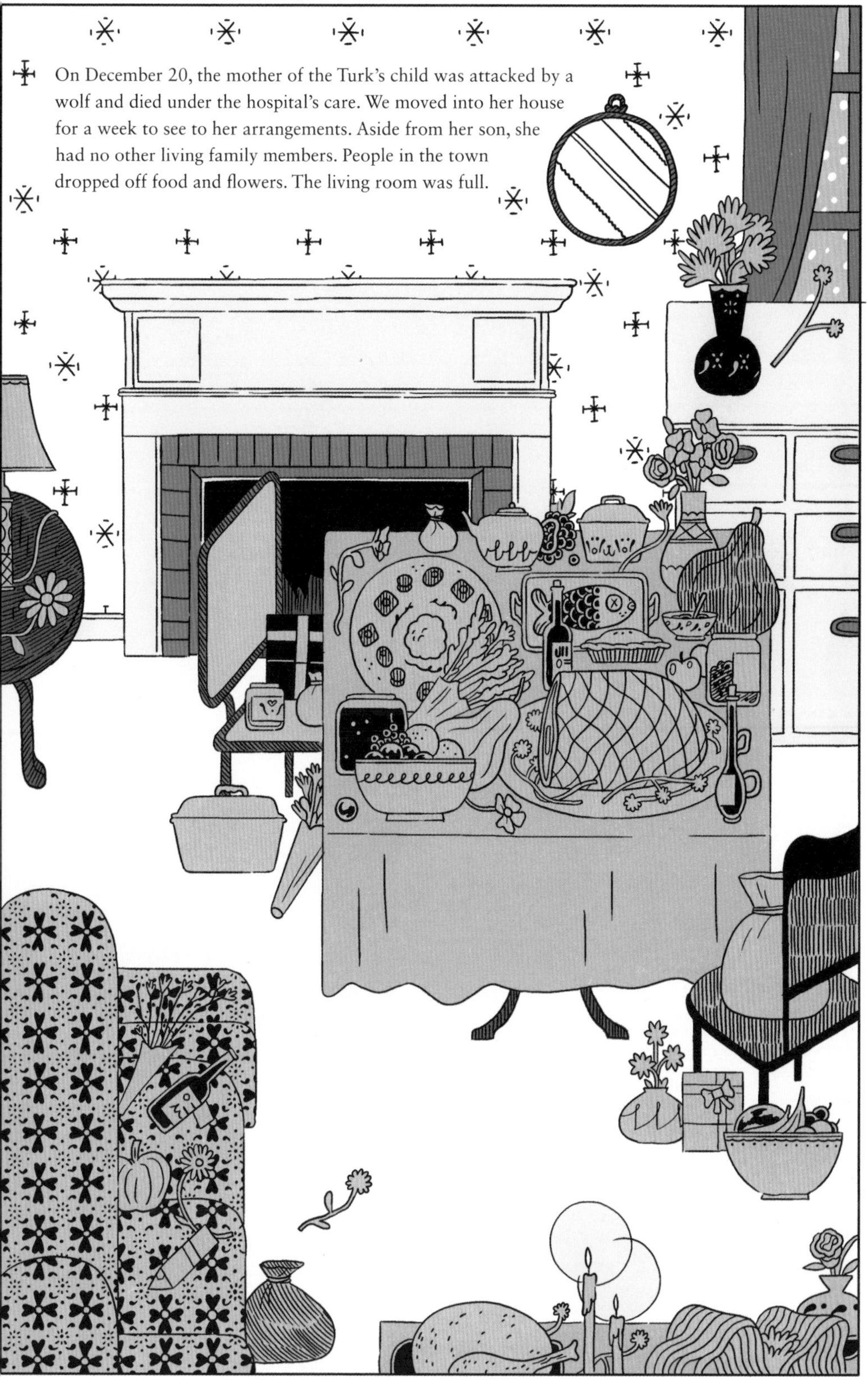
On December 20, the mother of the Turk's child was attacked by a wolf and died under the hospital's care. We moved into her house for a week to see to her arrangements. Aside from her son, she had no other living family members. People in the town dropped off food and flowers. The living room was full.

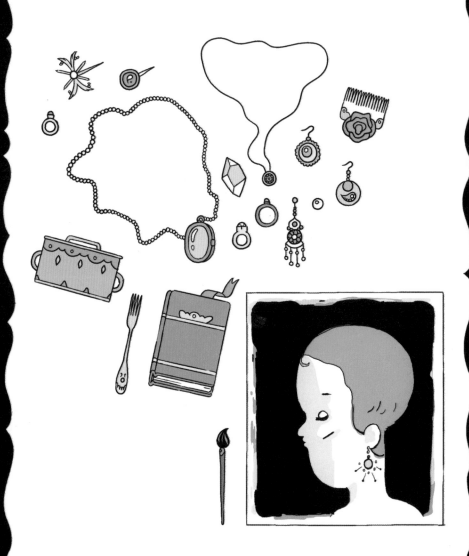

I was in charge of sorting through all her receipts, journals, and correspondence. She apparently had very little money to her name in the end, and she left behind a number of debts. I got in touch with anyone she still owed money to and repaid them with items from her personal inventory: jewelry, keepsakes, books, paintings she had made, furniture...anything I could find. I wrapped them like Christmas presents.

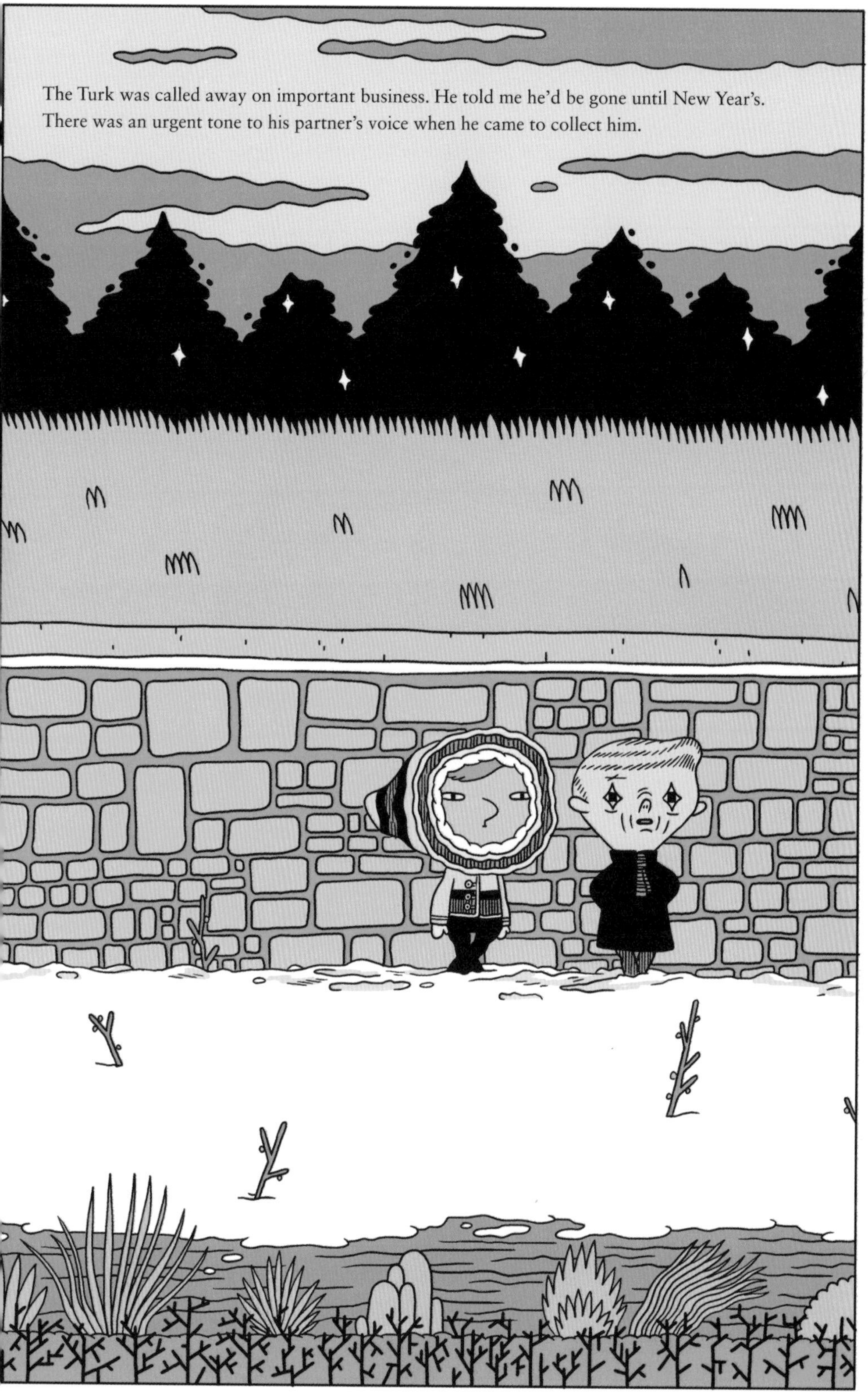
The Turk was called away on important business. He told me he'd be gone until New Year's. There was an urgent tone to his partner's voice when he came to collect him.

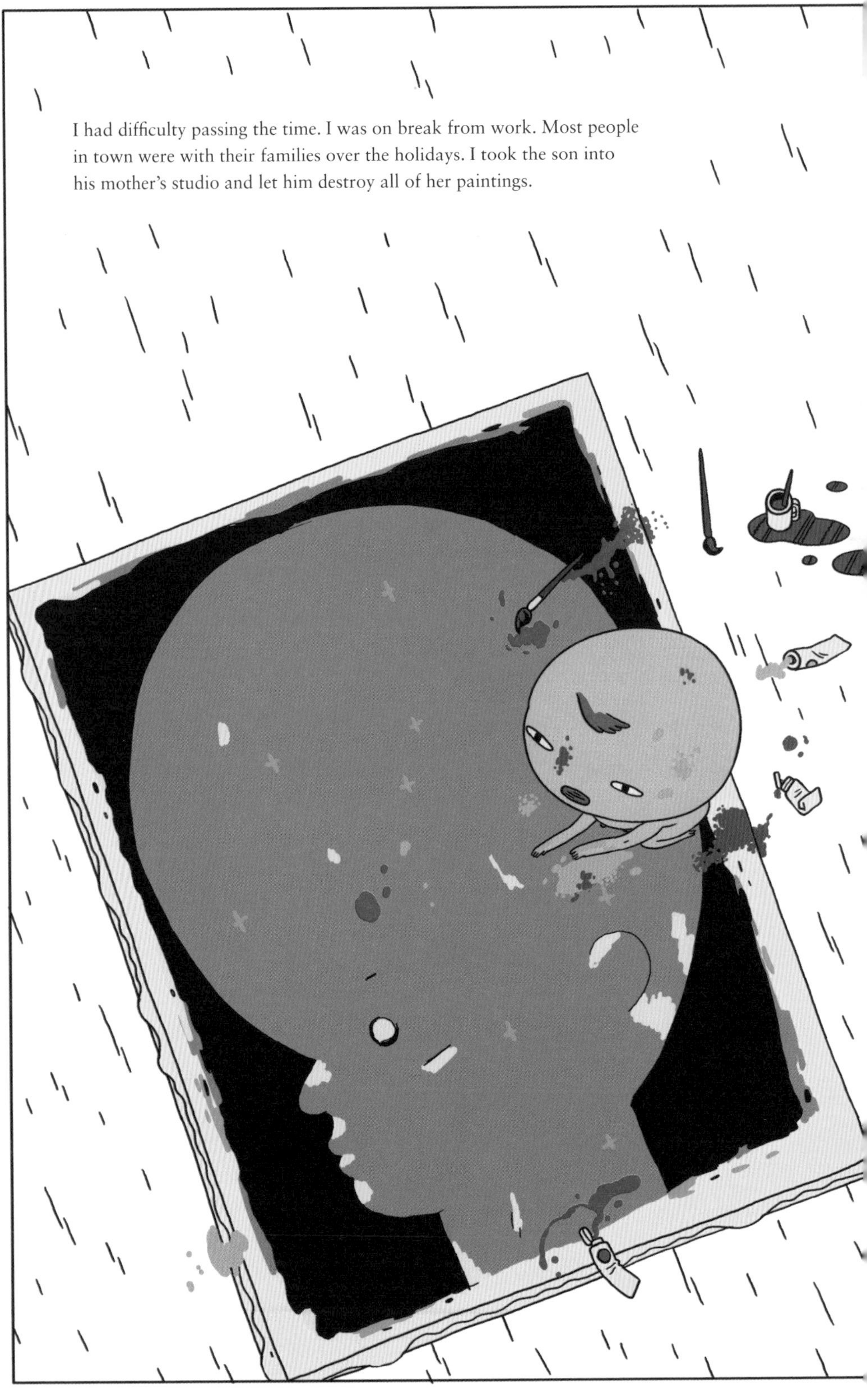
I had difficulty passing the time. I was on break from work. Most people in town were with their families over the holidays. I took the son into his mother's studio and let him destroy all of her paintings.

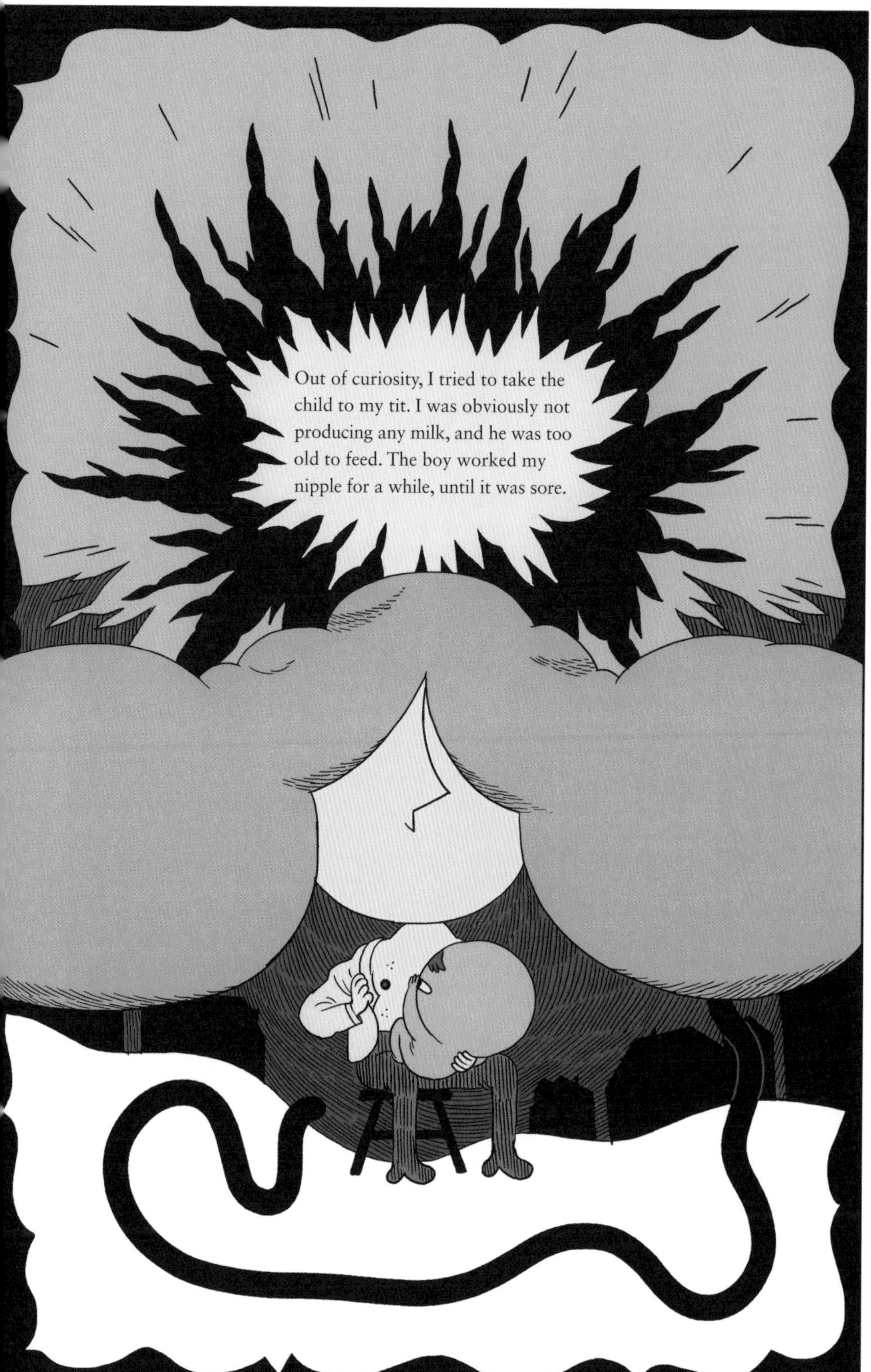
Out of curiosity, I tried to take the child to my tit. I was obviously not producing any milk, and he was too old to feed. The boy worked my nipple for a while, until it was sore.

It seemed impossible to fill the hours. I wondered how the woman did it. She made her living as a painter, which didn't seem like real work to me. To spend the entire day focused only on leisure? She must have been very bored.

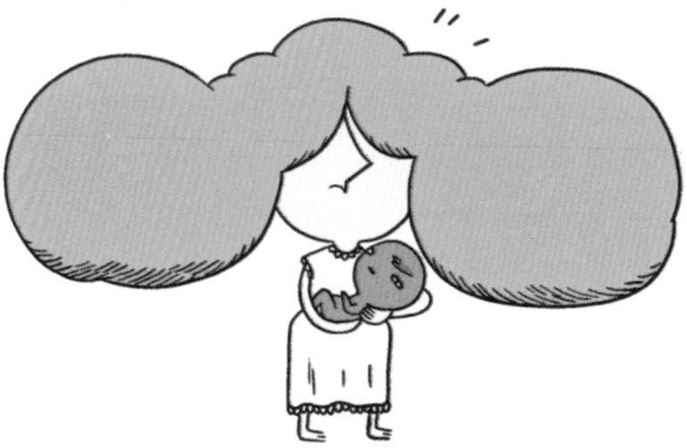

On the morning of the twenty-fourth, I walked down the stairs to find the Turk's partner sitting in the living room, pointing a gun at me. He was asking where the Turk was. I had no idea, of course.

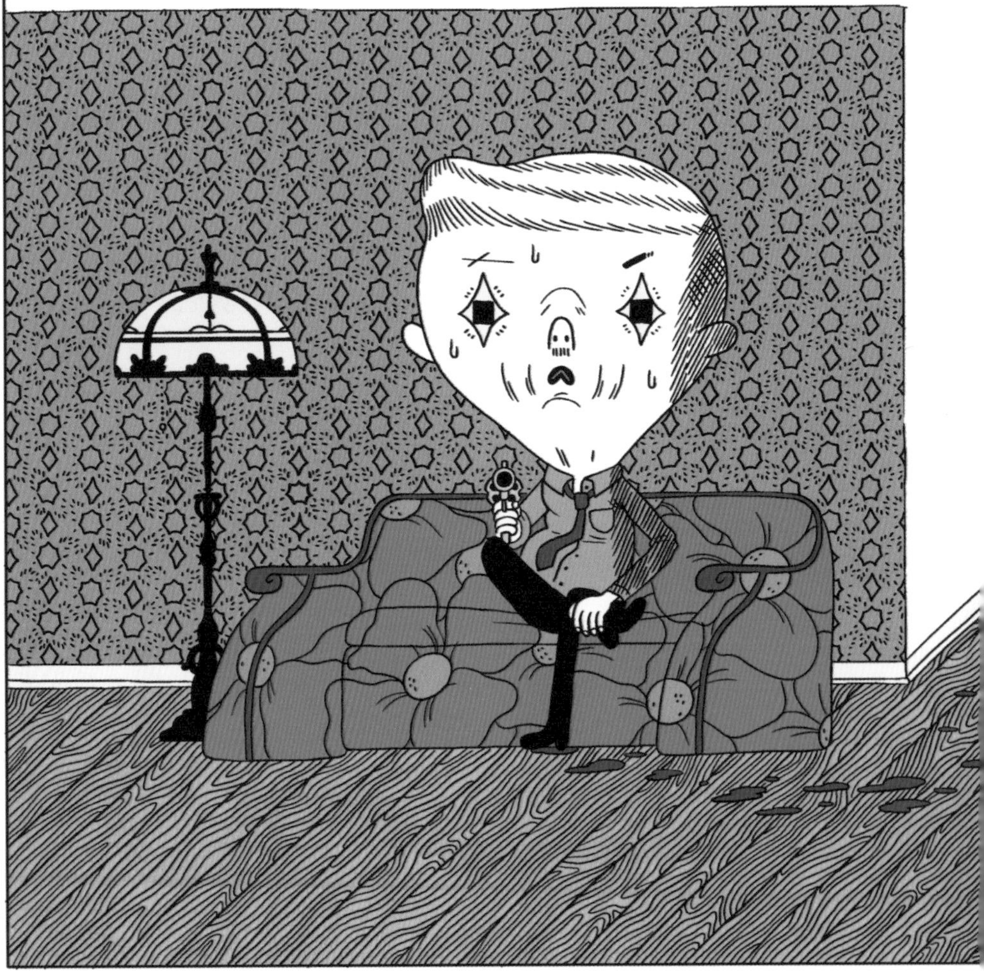

He looked panicked. He told me that if I left the living room, he'd shoot me down. He said he would wait there until the Turk either returned home or phoned in.

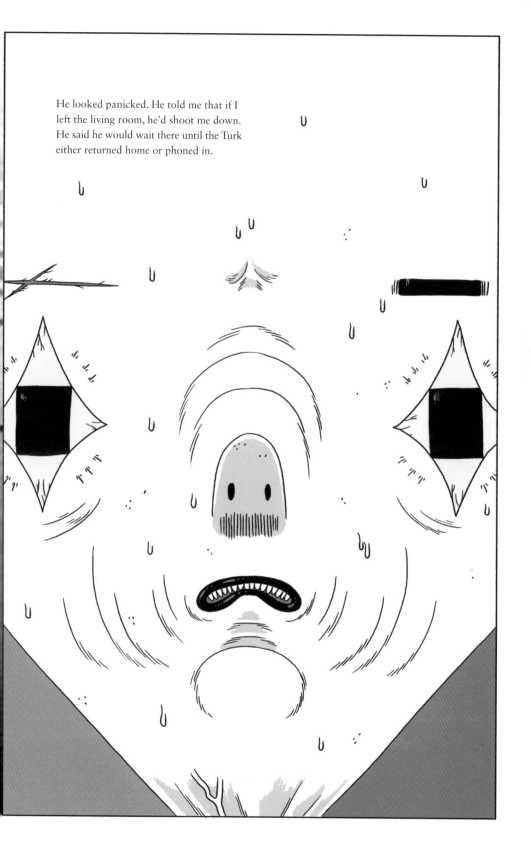

Hours passed. We spent this time together in almost complete silence. We eventually started eating some of the food the townspeople had left. He kept his gun fixed on me throughout the meal.

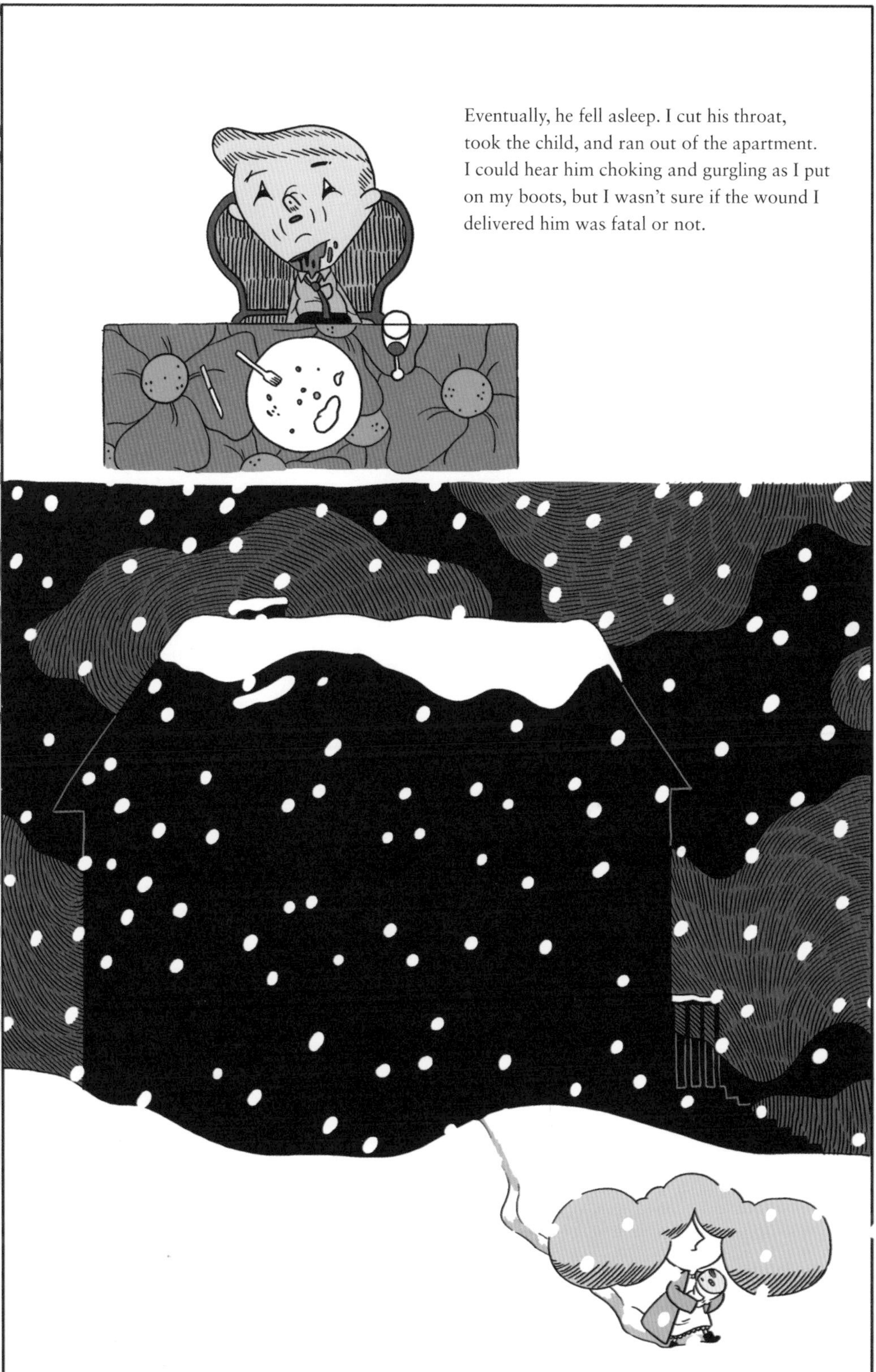
Eventually, he fell asleep. I cut his throat, took the child, and ran out of the apartment. I could hear him choking and gurgling as I put on my boots, but I wasn't sure if the wound I delivered him was fatal or not.

I called out for help. I could see my neighbours' lights turn on and could see them observing me from their windows. Nobody left their house. Eventually, each light would flicker off.

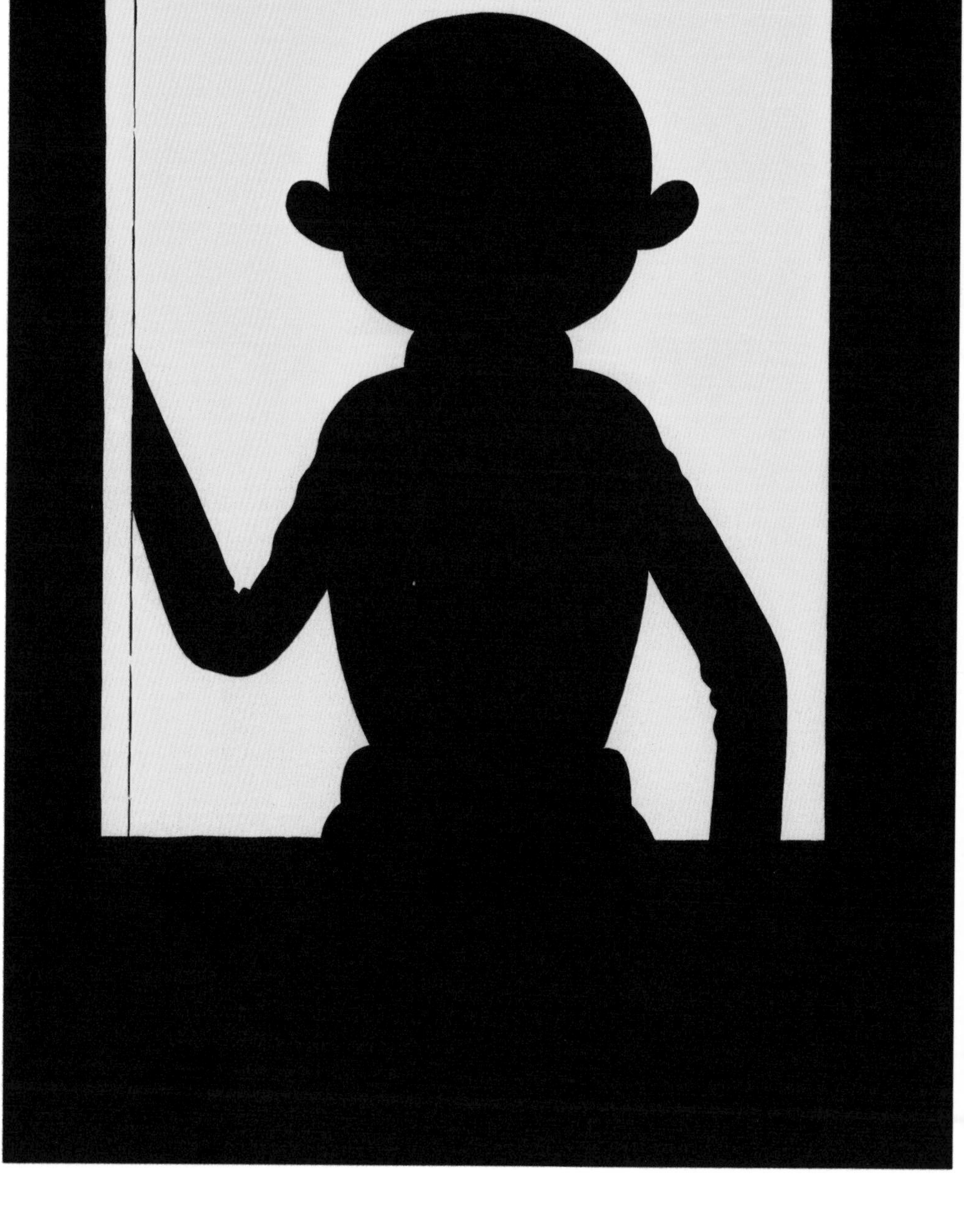

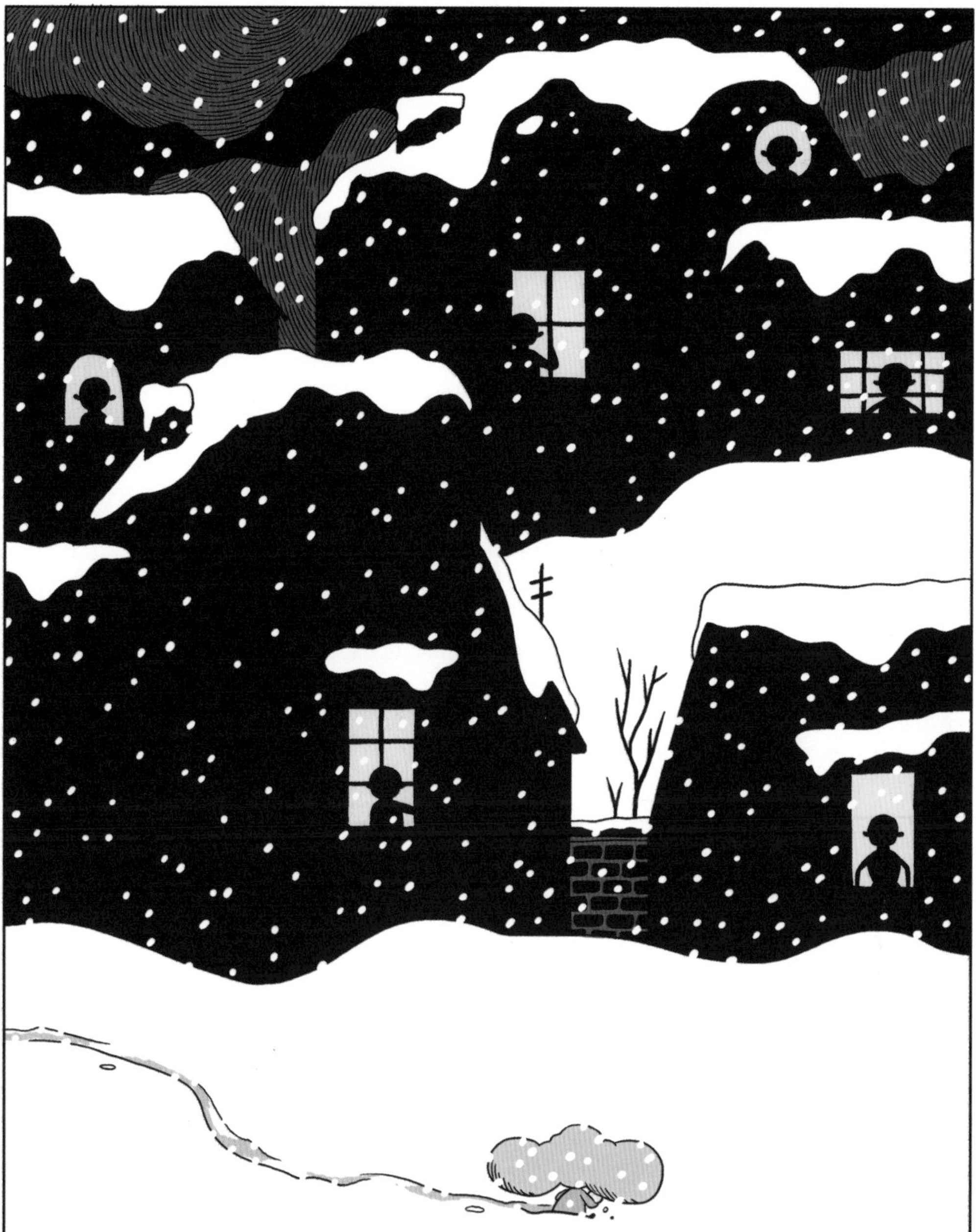

I wondered if they assumed I was just having another episode. Other patients in the hospital had warned me about this. After the first time, people would want to help. They'd be sympathetic. But a relapse would be met with revulsion—anger, even. They'd grow weary of me.

I thought about running to one of my brothers' houses, but in my exhausted, delirious, and illogical state, I decided against it. I pictured them enjoying Christmas Eve together with their families. In that moment, the thought of interrupting them seemed insurmountably horrible. In the year I'd been back from the hospital, my brothers never introduced me to their wives or children. It only occurred to me that night that there might have been a reason for this.

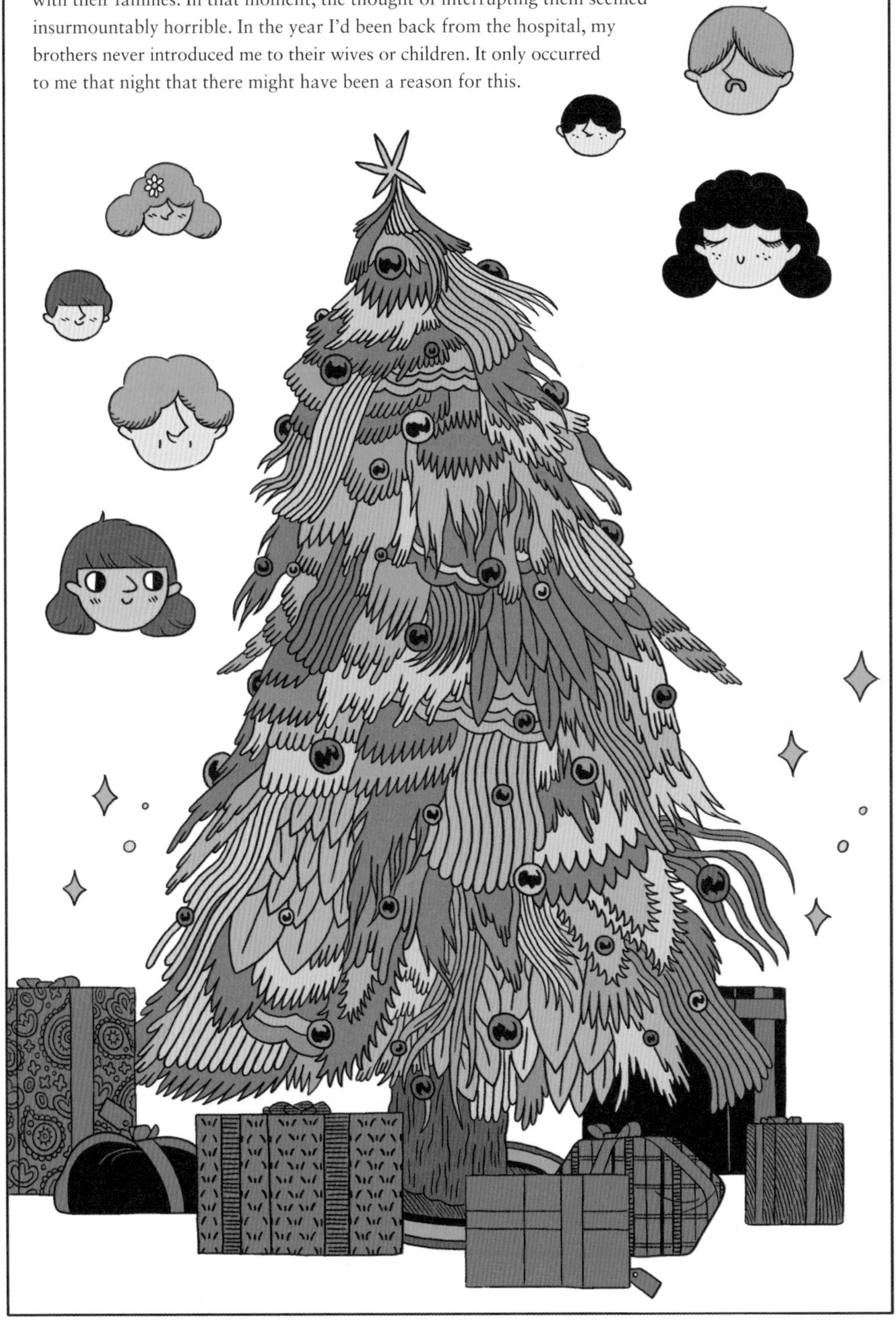

Not knowing what else to do, I walked back to the house. To my surprise, the intruder was gone. There was a stain on the floor where his body must have collapsed, but no trail of blood indicating that he had crawled somewhere else to either escape or die.

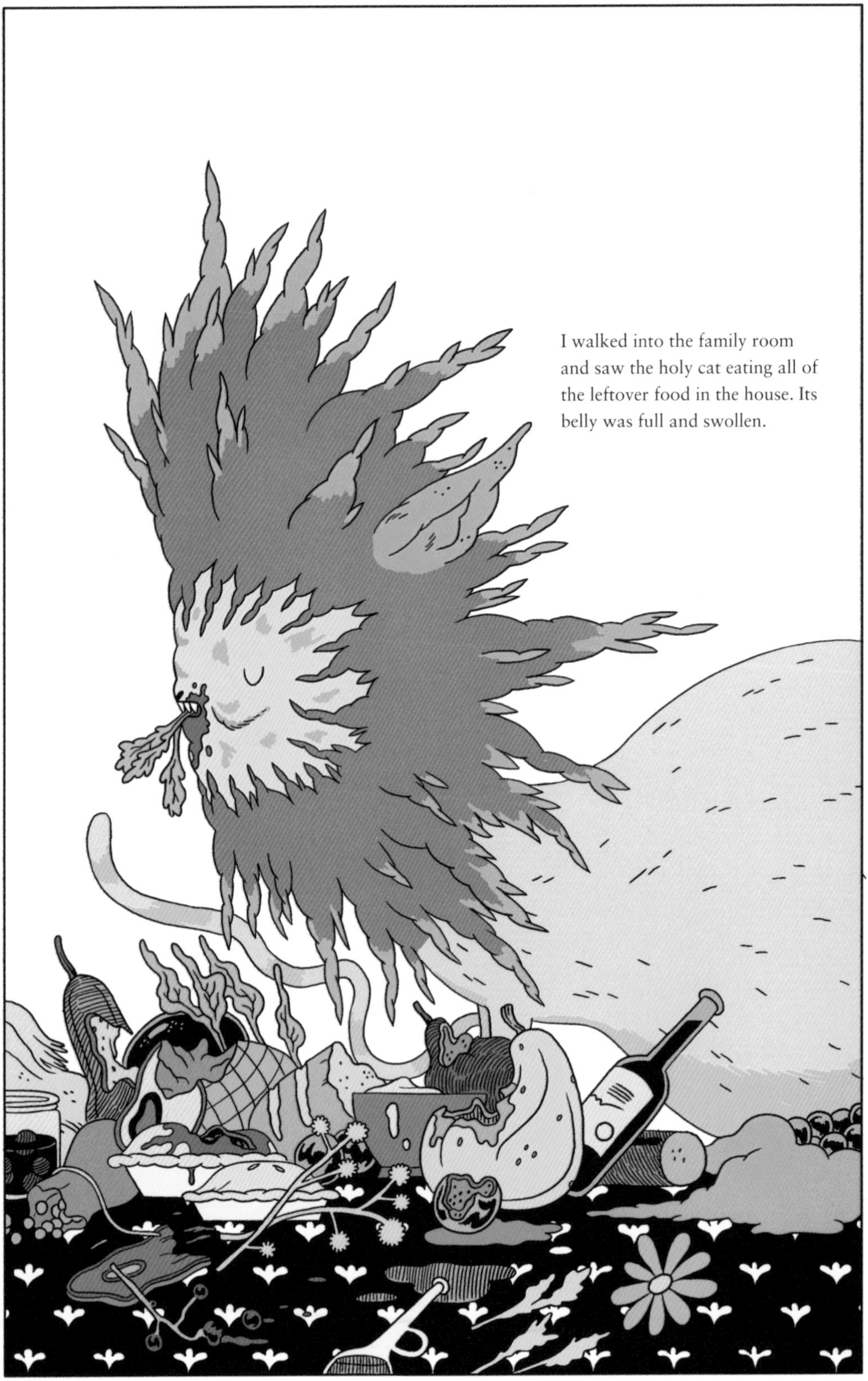
I walked into the family room and saw the holy cat eating all of the leftover food in the house. Its belly was full and swollen.

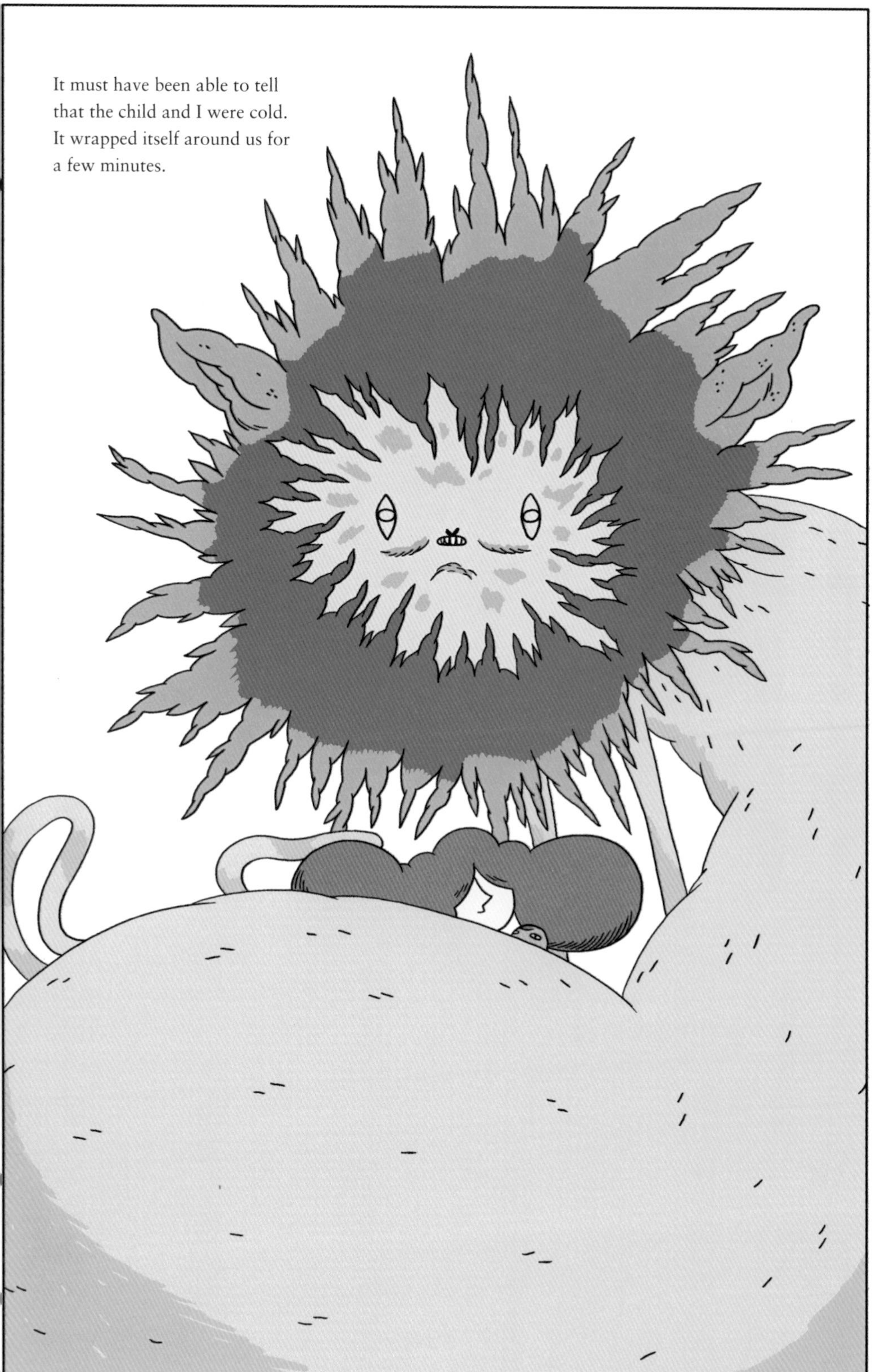
It must have been able to tell that the child and I were cold. It wrapped itself around us for a few minutes.

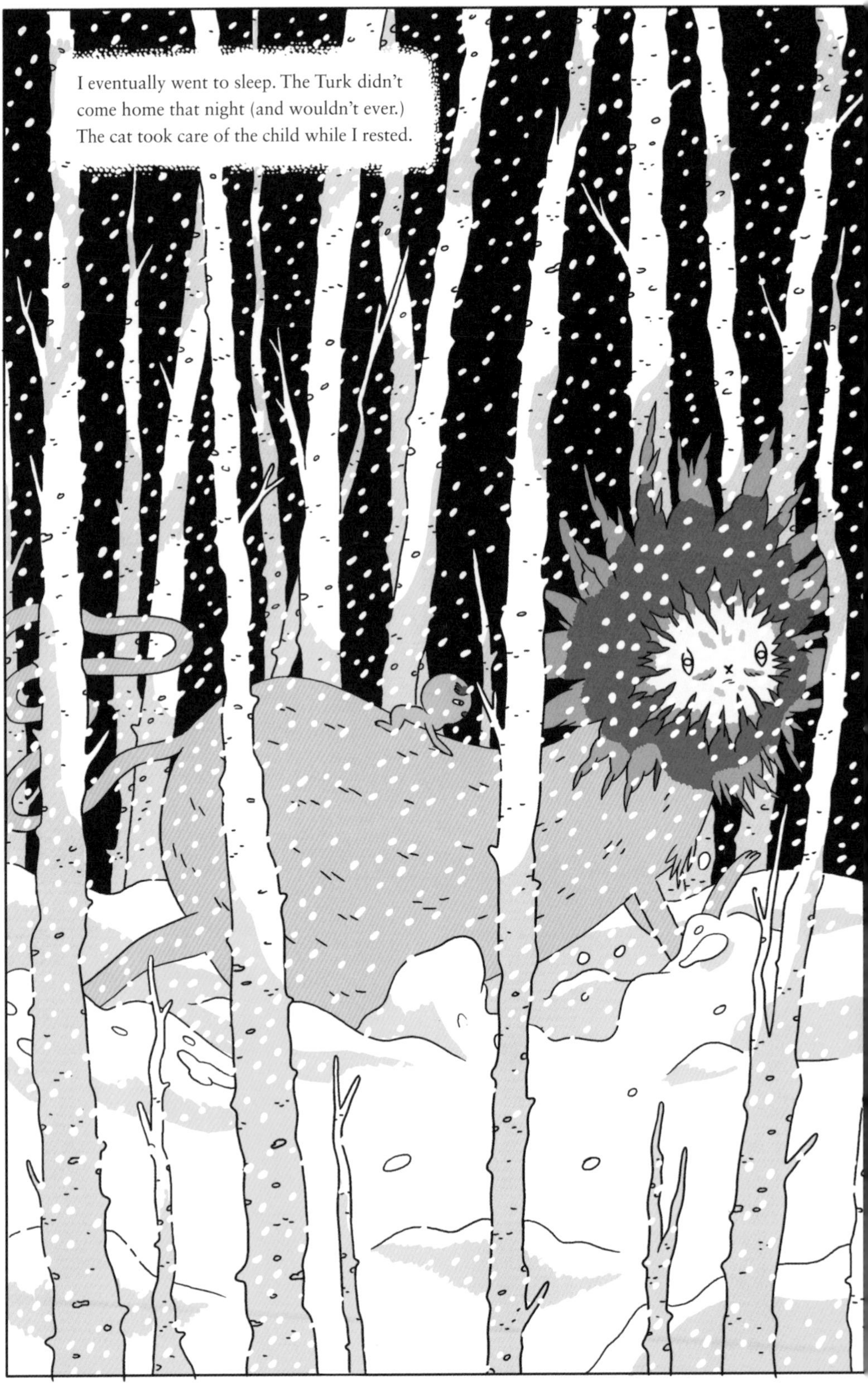
I eventually went to sleep. The Turk didn't come home that night (and wouldn't ever.) The cat took care of the child while I rested.

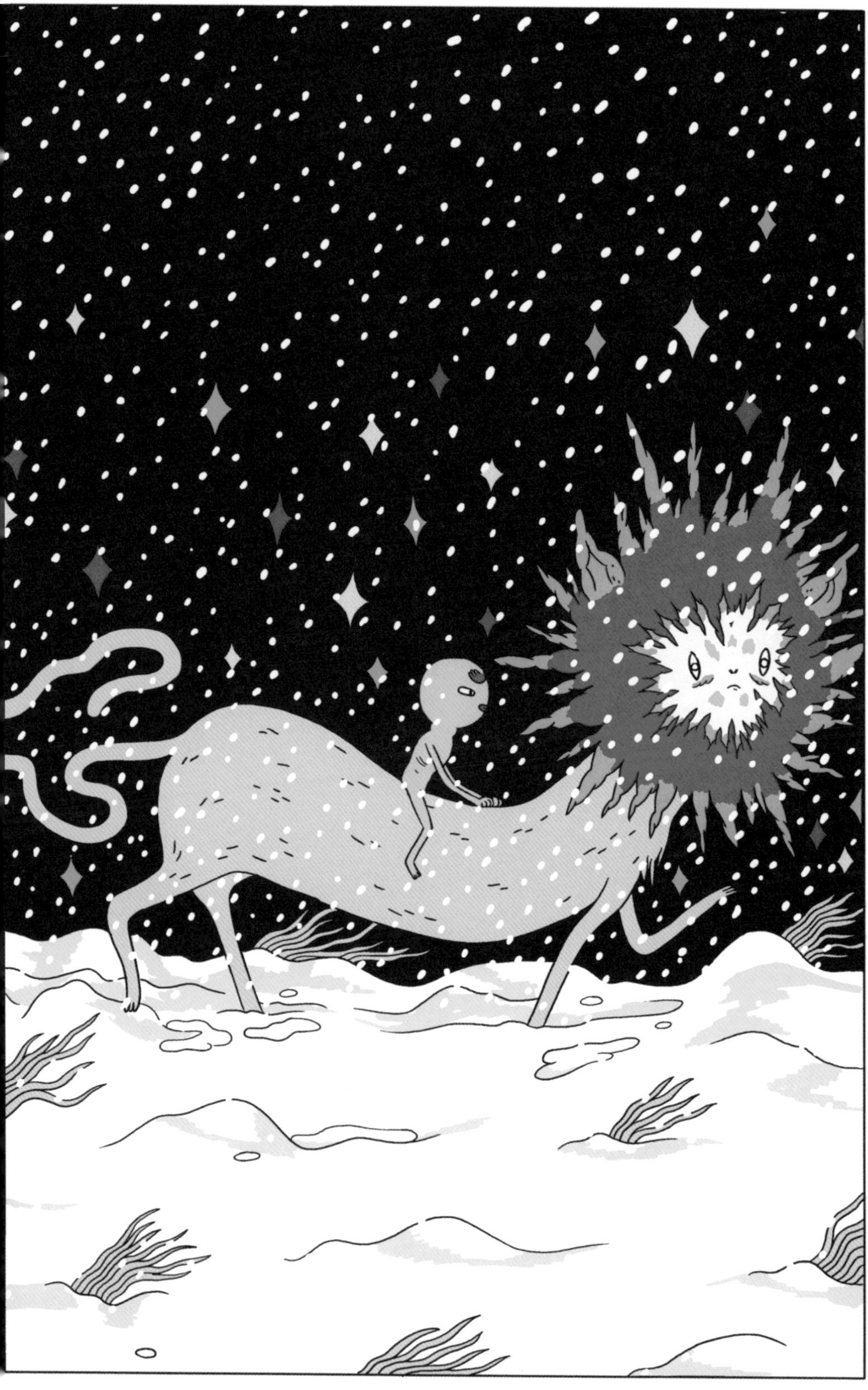

Thanks to everyone at Drawn & Quarterly,
Leslie, Ryan, Patrick, Ginette, Robin, Anne, and my family.

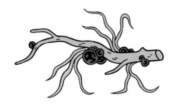

drawnandquarterly.com / kingtrash.com

First hardcover edition: January 2014. Printed in Malaysia. 10   9   8   7   6   5   4   3   2   1

Drawn & Quarterly acknowledges the financial contribution of the Government of Canada through the Canada Book Fund and the Canada Council for the Arts for our publishing activities and for support of this edition.

Library and Archives Canada Cataloguing in Publication: DeForge, Michael, 1987–, author, illustrator. *First Year Healthy* / Michael DeForge. ISBN 978-1-77046-173-4 (bound). 1. Graphic novels. I. Title. PN6733. D435F57 2015   741.5'971   C2014-903568-3

Published in the USA by Drawn & Quarterly, a client publisher of *Farrar, Straus and Giroux*. Orders: 888.330.8477
Published in Canada by Drawn & Quarterly, a client publisher of *Raincoast Books*. Orders: 800.663.5714
Published in the UK by Drawn & Quarterly, a client publisher of *Publishers Group UK*. Orders: info@pguk.co.uk

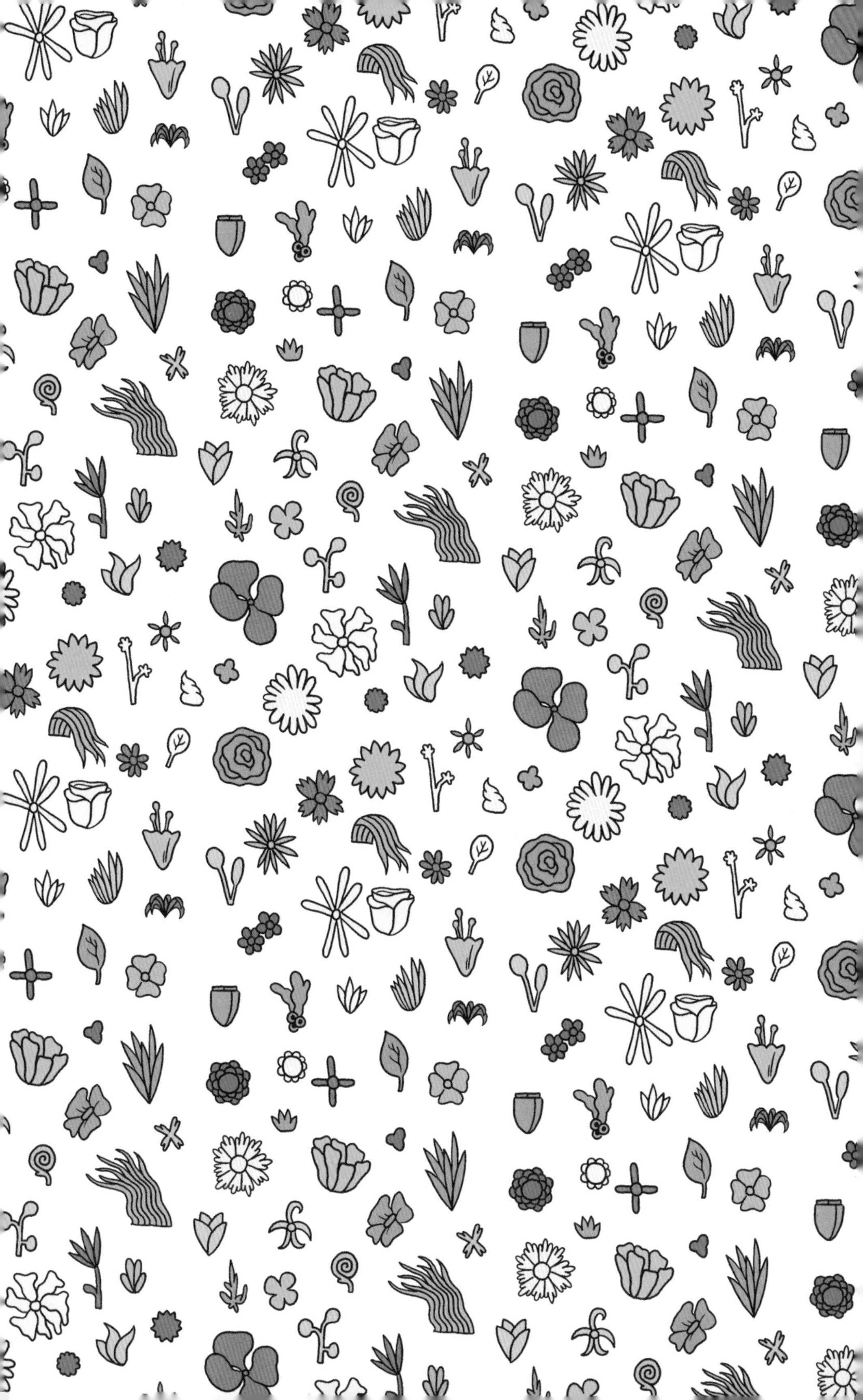

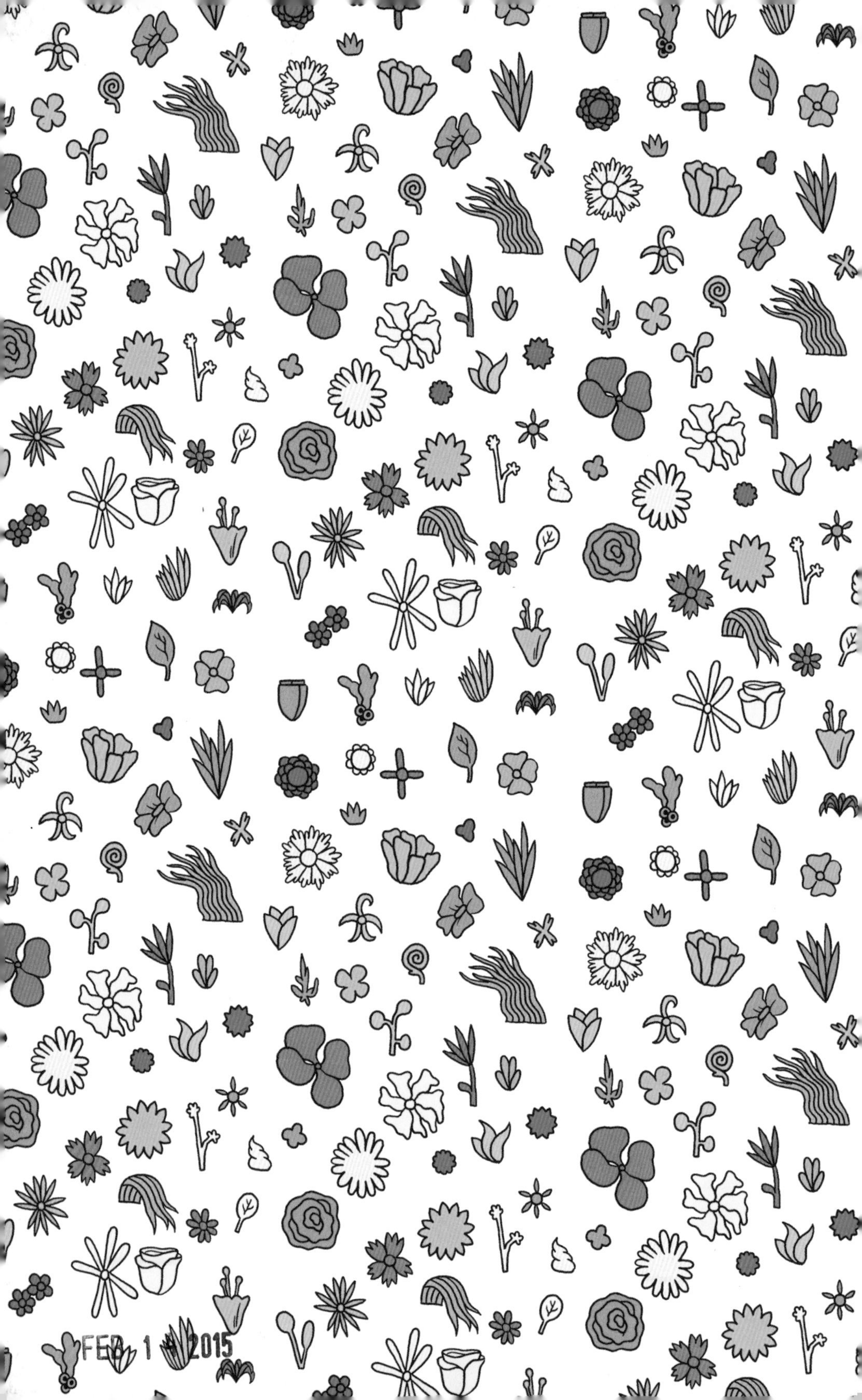